Soil

All soils are improved by the addition of well rotted animal manure, composted vegetation and peat. Very heavy soils are made much easier to dig and hoe if peat and compost is worked into them. Don't scatter a little peat or compost over a big area – that way you never get the benefit. Concentrate the application in one spot up to three inches deep and gradually improve the whole plot, then you will really see the improvement very quickly.

Organic matter holds moisture in light soils, improves the drainage in heavier soils and encourages root growth in all soils.

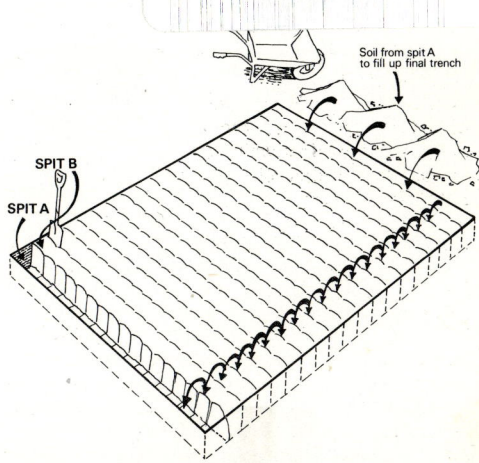

Soil from spit A to fill up final trench

SPIT B

SPIT A

Digging over the plot

Digging the soil to a 'spades' depth

Digging is not the painfully hard job people expect if a comfortable, clean spade is used and a little soil is moved at a time. Take out a trench the width and depth of a spade at one end of the plot, piling the soil in a heap at the other end. Turn over a 3–4 inch wide strip of soil one spade deep across the plot, move back, do another 3–4 inch strip and so on, gently working over the plot. A layer of peat on wet soil keeps the feet clean and makes the digging even easier. Any annual weeds, the kinds without thick perennial roots, can be buried with the digging. Be sure to pick out the perennial roots as you go to avoid a lot of weed hoeing next year.

Leave the spadefuls of soil in big lumps when digging in the autumn, the frost will break it down into crumbly pieces. When digging in spring break the lumps down to prevent soil drying into large clods. Aim to dig at a time when a few hours dry weather will follow. Rain immediately after digging prevents the desired crumbly structure being formed, especially on heavy, wet soil.

Plant Feeding and Composting

We recommend a scattering of general fertiliser, Growmore or any of the proprietary general garden products, in spring and the use of some liquid fertiliser as a ginger up for some crops in the summer. Rose or tomato fertiliser can replace Growmore if the crops require more potash (see respective crop notes). Bonfire ash is another good source of potash. *Never* exceed the fertiliser dose, there is nothing to be gained and excessive fertiliser damages rather than improves growth.

The most important constituent of rich and fertile soils is the organic matter and here the addition of more organic matter is entirely in the gardener's hands. Why not tidy up the garden, all the old non-woody plant material, the kitchen waste, the lawn mowings and the leaves into a compost heap? Here is the way to do it. First, four canes, pieces of pipe or stakes 4 feet long are put 1 foot into the ground to mark out a rectangle at least 3′ × 5′. Surround the canes with wire or plastic netting, pieces of corrugated iron, anything to make four sides 3 feet high. Then pile in all the green plant waste. If your children keep rabbits or similar pets, bed them on dry peat and the hutch cleanings can be added to the compost to speed the rotting down process. If you have no animal manure a good sprinkling of proprietary compost maker is needed every now and again.

Starting in early summer, there will be quite a heap the following early spring when the four stakes can be taken out and re-erected round an adjacent rectangle. Take the netting and put this round the new position and turn the accumulated heap top to bottom into this and leave for a week or two to settle. Then take the stakes and sides down again and erect in the original position for the next collection of material for rotting. Once well rotted down this compost is ideal for mulching all fruit crops.

COMPOST BIN B
EARLY SPRING-YEAR 2

COMPOST BIN A
SUMMER-YEAR 1

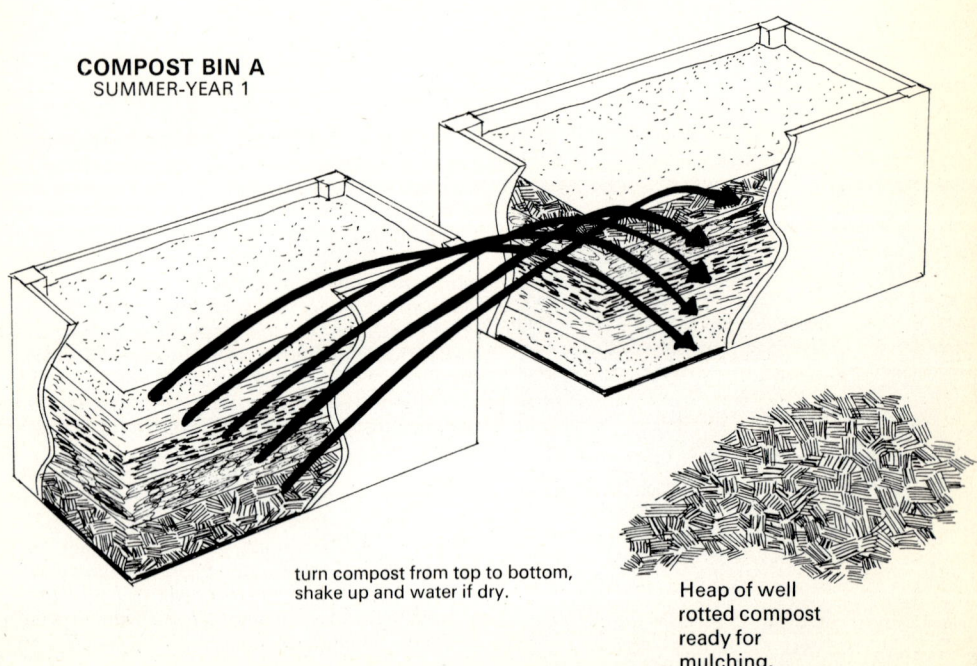

turn compost from top to bottom, shake up and water if dry.

Heap of well rotted compost ready for mulching.

Choice of Site

An open, sunny site protected from strong cold winds is the ideal for fruit growing. Where large trees and buildings close the site in and throw dense shadows cropping is still possible, although fruits like apricots, peaches and the more temperamental varieties of pears are best omitted.

Strong cold winds are a problem in spring when the plants are in flower because they prevent the activities of pollinating insects. Fortunately many suburban gardens are surrounded by hedges, fences and walls which give considerable protection.

Where the selected plot is fenced on two or three sides this is an advantage when it comes to erecting some form of netting to protect your plants against birds — pecking fruit buds in the winter and pecking the ripe fruit in summer. The side fences are also valuable for trailing cane fruits, trained bushes and trees.

Detailed Cropping Plan

This detailed cropping plan packs the maximum into our limited area. It will be necessary to thin out some of the soft fruit as the different kinds grow and demand more space. Cropping in this way is not new, commercial growers have for years under-cropped newly planted trees with soft fruits to provide earlier cash returns. The soft fruits are reduced and removed as the trees produce a deep overhead canopy.

There are, of course, countless different fruit combinations which can be used and this plan offers a framework from which to start. The two trees ideally need to be to the north of the plot, they can equally well be plums and pears although apples on dwarfing roots which keep them compact are likely to be the easiest to handle.

Any of the wall and fence trained vines, cane and cordon fruits can be planted around the perimeter. The family may prefer loganberries to other fruits for example and all three sides

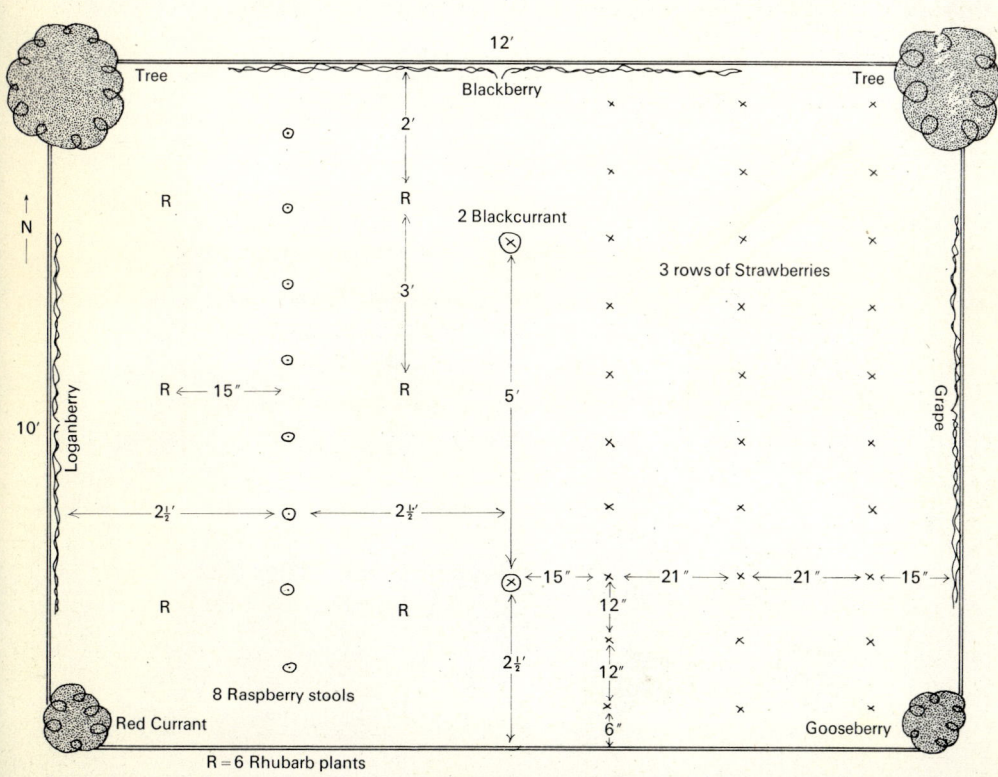

could be furnished with logan-berries. Grapes will require warm conditions for the best quality fruit and the cane fruits would be better in colder northern districts.

After three and to a maximum of five years the strawberries would need replacing by new plants. In this plan we would see the area cleared of strawberries either taken up by the increasing size of black-currants or replanted with rhubarb. It may be possible to replant a few strawberries in the area previously cropped by rhubarb. The raspberries and soft fruits would need to be kept pruned back and canes tied in well to allow enough light to get through to the strawberries.

Growing the redcurrant and gooseberry bushes on a taller stem, 2–2½ feet high, would give more space for this subsequent strawberry and rhubarb planting.

Simplified Plan

It will be easier to grow more of less varieties and those people new to fruit gardening may prefer to start off with this simplified plan. After cropping with strawberries and rhubarb for 6–10 years it would be as well to change over plots, moving fruit to vegetable and vice versa. This would give an acceptable rotation of crops and reduce the likelihood of soil borne disease build up.

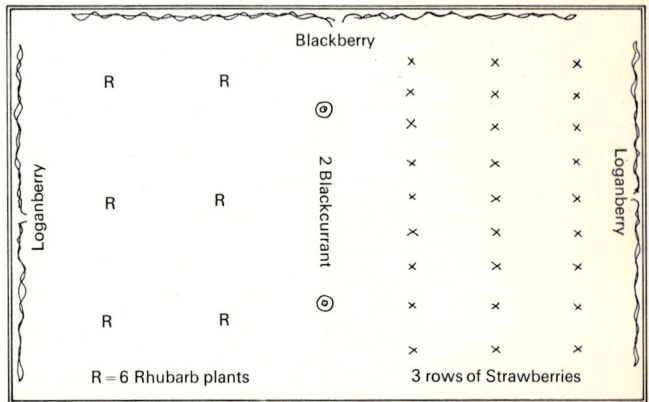

The absence of raspberries, which will grow some 6 feet (2 m) high and trees makes netting over much easier where three sides are protected with interwoven and similar fencing.

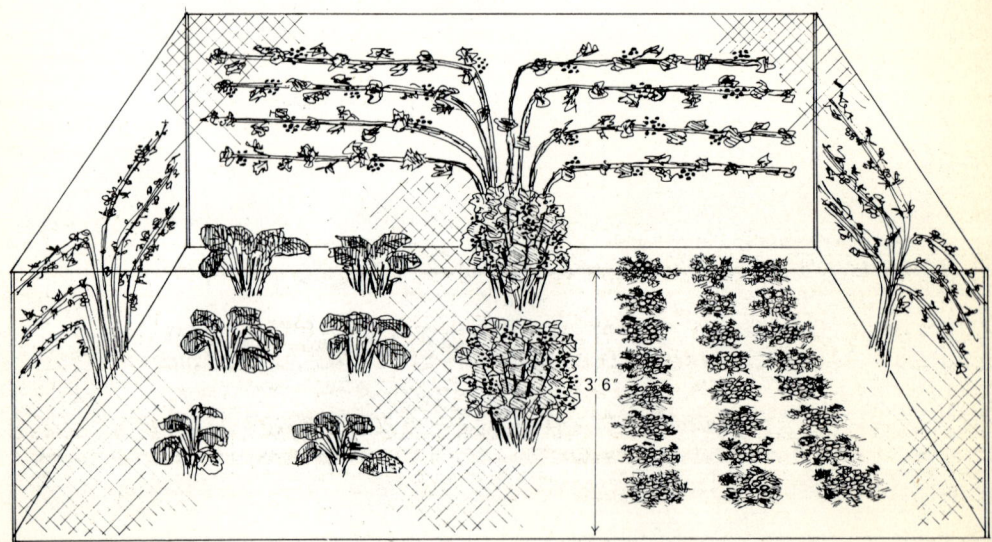

Year~Round Fresh Fruit Supply Chart

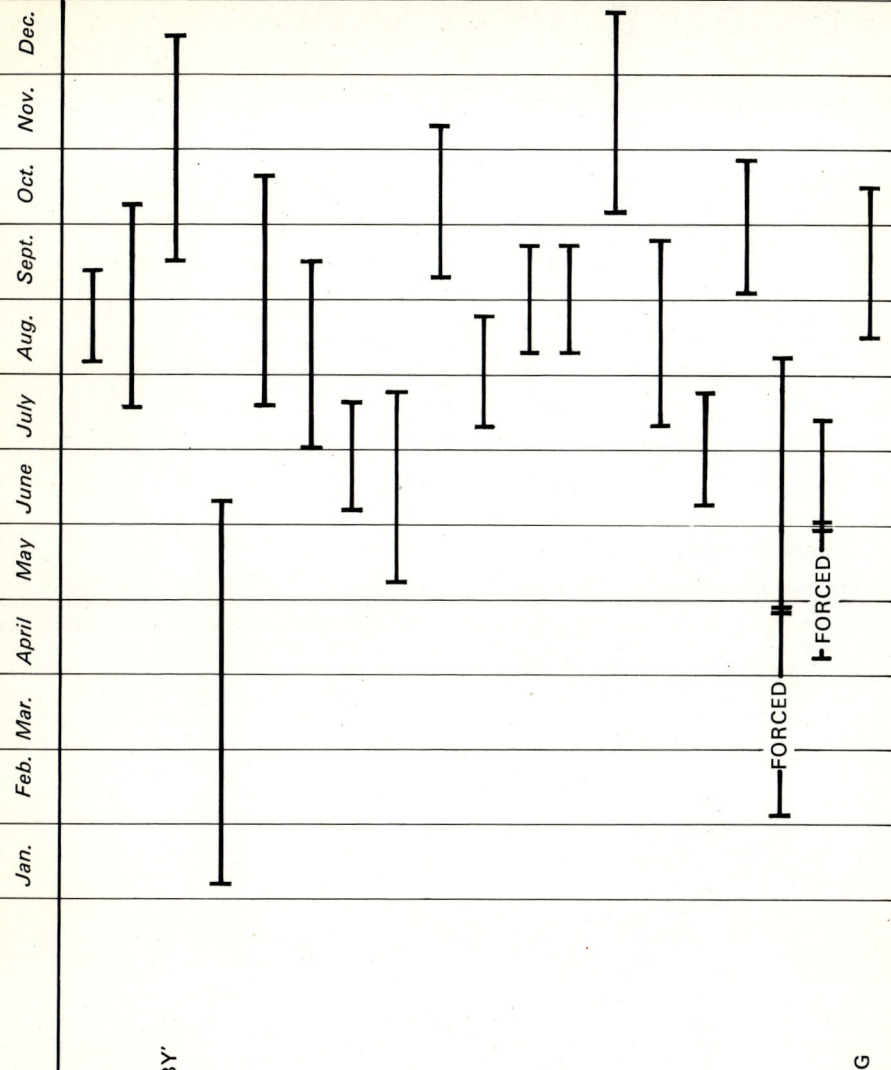

	Jan.	Feb.	Mar.	April	May	June	July	Aug.	Sept.	Oct.	Nov.	Dec.
APRICOT												
APPLE EARLY e.g. 'GRENADIER'												
APPLE MID SEASON e.g. 'LORD DERBY'												
APPLE LATE e.g. 'IDARED'												
BLACKBERRY IN VARIETY												
CHERRIES												
CURRANTS												
GOOSEBERRIES												
GRAPES												
LOGANBERRIES												
PEACHES												
PEARS EARLY												
PEARS LATE												
PLUMS												
RASPBERRIES												
RASPBERRIES AUTUMN FRUITING												
RHUBARB		FORCED										
STRAWBERRIES				FORCED								
STRAWBERRIES PERPETUAL FRUITING												

7

Training for Shape

There is quite a variety of ways we can train the growth of fruiting plants to suit the smaller garden. The easiest is a *stool*, for example: blackberry, blackcurrant, blueberry, loganberry and raspberry.

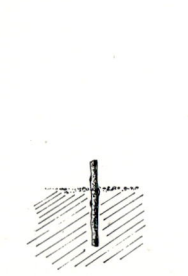 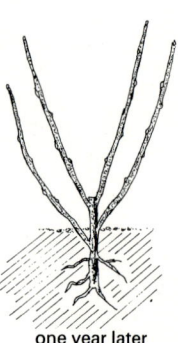 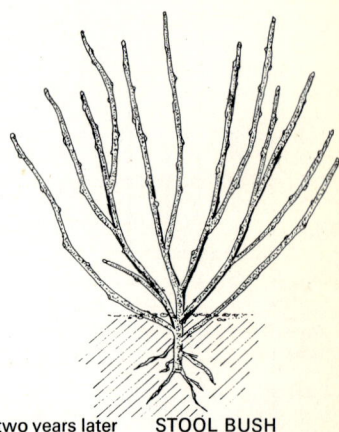

cutting autumn or rooted tip   one year later   two years later   STOOL BUSH

Pruning a young bush tree

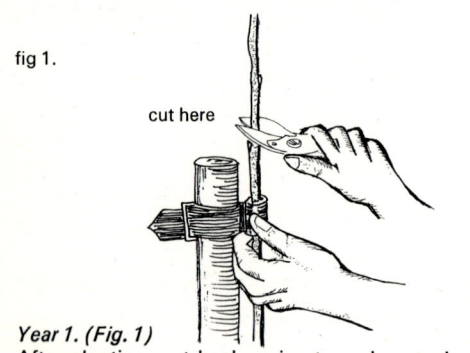

fig 1.

cut here

Year 1. (Fig. 1)
After planting, cut back main stem above a bud about 24 inches above soil level.

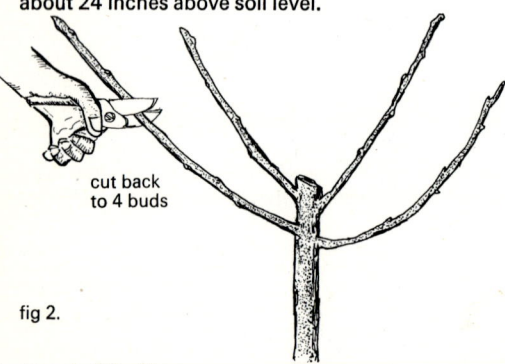

cut back to 4 buds

fig 2.

Year 2. (Fig. 2)
During winter, cut back all the strong new shoots by about half.

Soft fruits and figs are propagated from rooted cuttings and the tree fruit – sometimes called top-fruit – is either grafted or budded onto special roots. The plants grown as stools, no more than bushes with no trunk as such, require no branch and framework training, only routine pruning. Take the plant up on a small trunk to form a *bush* and we have the common way to grow: apricots, apples, cherries, figs, gooseberry, peaches, pears and redcurrants (see p.10) Fruit Tree Shapes.

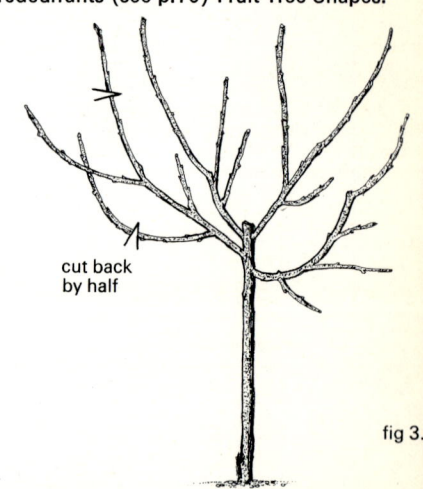

cut back by half

fig 3.

Year 3. (Fig. 3)
During winter, branches needed to continue the main framework are reduced by half. Side shoots which developed from the pruning in Year 2 are cut back to 4 buds.

Raise the stem height to form *half standards* and raise it further still to form *standards.*

Restricting the development of branches and training the plant to produce spurs (short multi-branched shoots which carry fruit each year) around a single stem is the way to grow cordons Apples and pears are the most commonly grown as *single cordons* (Page 11). It is also possible to have *two-* and *three-stemmed cordons* (see Gooseberry cordon p.39).
   Cordons are grown in one plane to produce a 'hedge' effect, supported either by wires on posts or against a wall. *(Fig 4)*

This flat method of training is provided with: *espalier* apples and pears (Page 11), where a single central stem supports pairs of horizontal branches; and *fan-shaped* (Page 11) trees suitable for all the tree fruits and especially those with stone fruits.

Pruning a young espalier

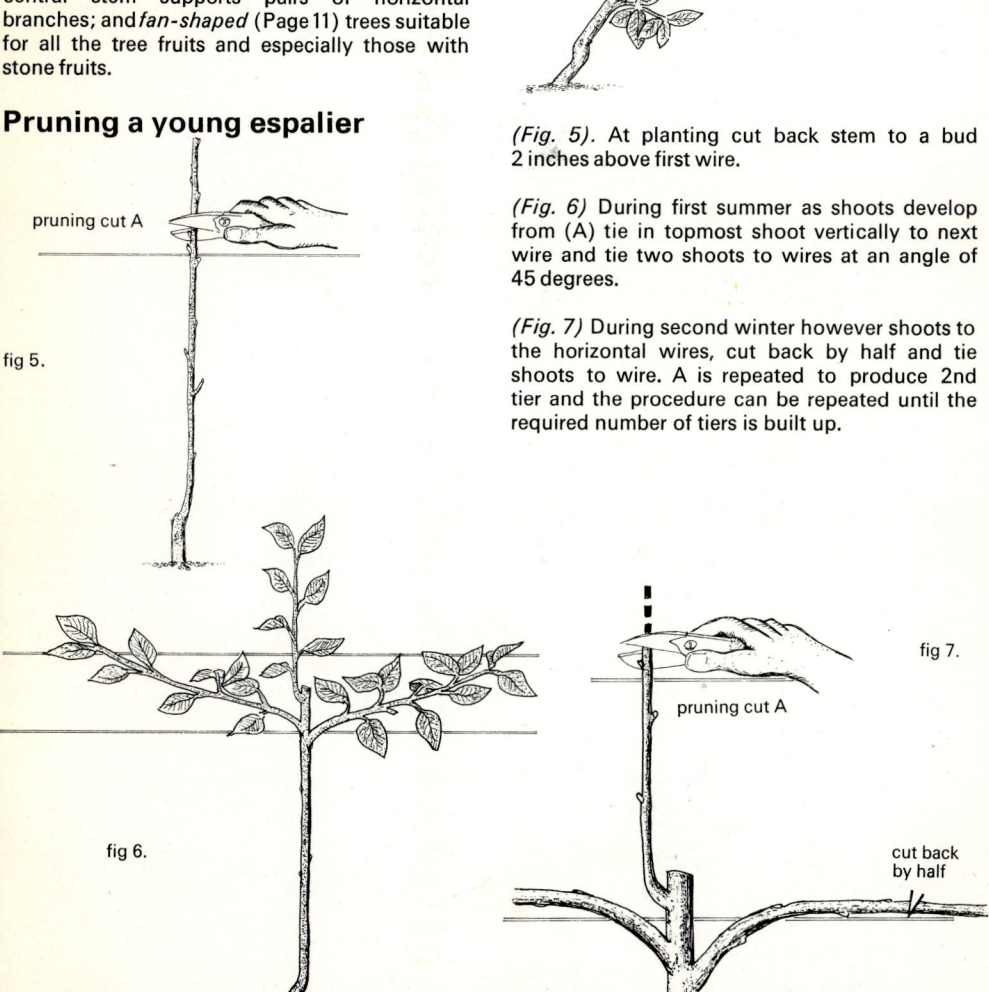

fig 4.

pruning cut A

fig 5.

fig 6.

fig 7.

pruning cut A

cut back by half

(Fig. 5). At planting cut back stem to a bud 2 inches above first wire.

(Fig. 6) During first summer as shoots develop from (A) tie in topmost shoot vertically to next wire and tie two shoots to wires at an angle of 45 degrees.

(Fig. 7) During second winter however shoots to the horizontal wires, cut back by half and tie shoots to wire. A is repeated to produce 2nd tier and the procedure can be repeated until the required number of tiers is built up.

FRUIT TREE SHAPES

Fruit trees can usually be purchased from a
garden centre with the basic framework established

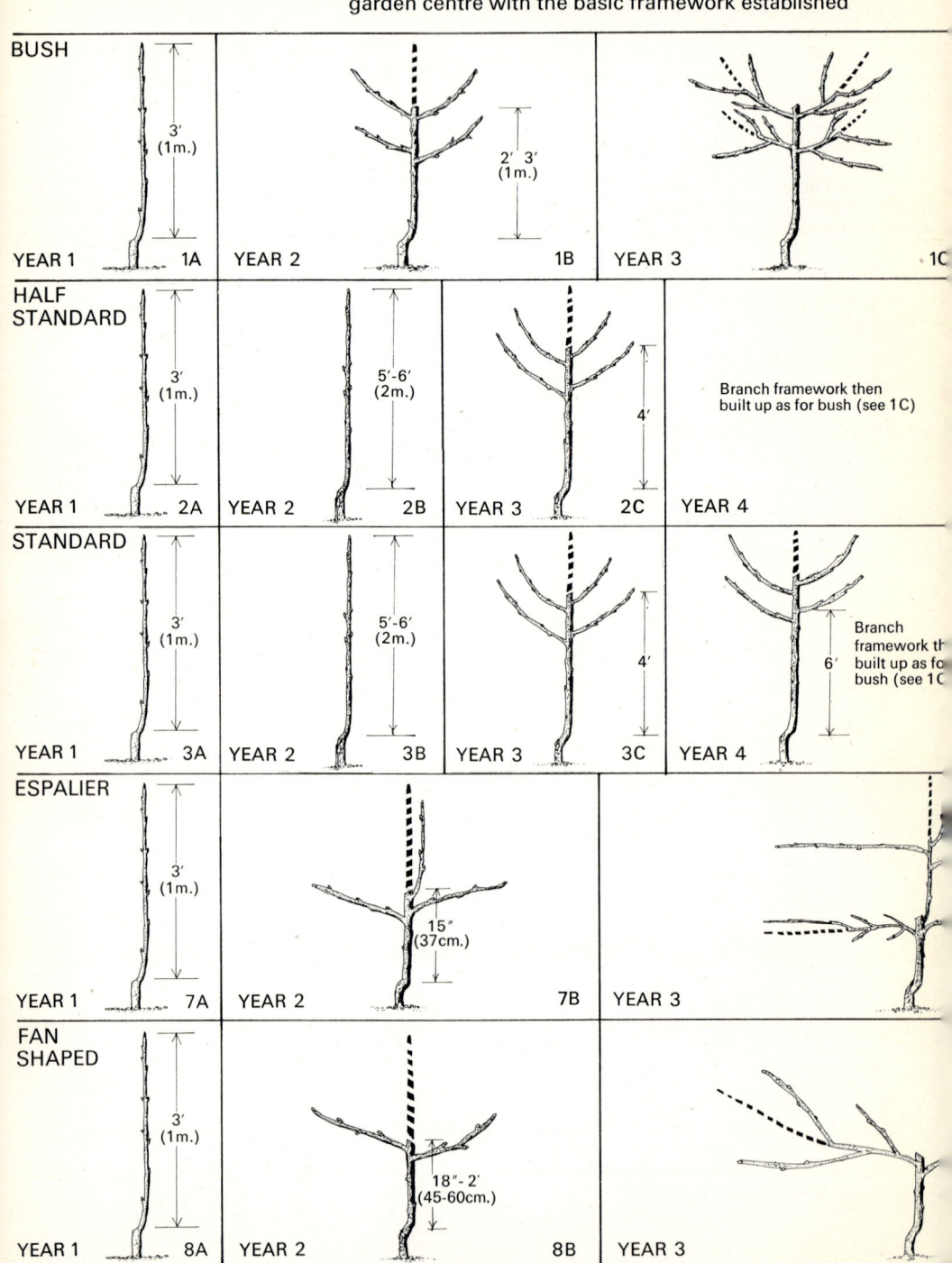

BUSH

YEAR 1 — 3' (1m.) — 1A

YEAR 2 — 2' 3' (1m.) — 1B

YEAR 3 — 1C

HALF STANDARD

YEAR 1 — 3' (1m.) — 2A

YEAR 2 — 5'-6' (2m.) — 2B

YEAR 3 — 4' — 2C

YEAR 4 — Branch framework then built up as for bush (see 1C)

STANDARD

YEAR 1 — 3' (1m.) — 3A

YEAR 2 — 5'-6' (2m.) — 3B

YEAR 3 — 4' — 3C

YEAR 4 — 6' — Branch framework th built up as fo bush (see 1C

ESPALIER

YEAR 1 — 3' (1m.) — 7A

YEAR 2 — 15" (37cm.) — 7B

YEAR 3

FAN SHAPED

YEAR 1 — 3' (1m.) — 8A

YEAR 2 — 18"- 2' (45-60cm.) — 8B

YEAR 3

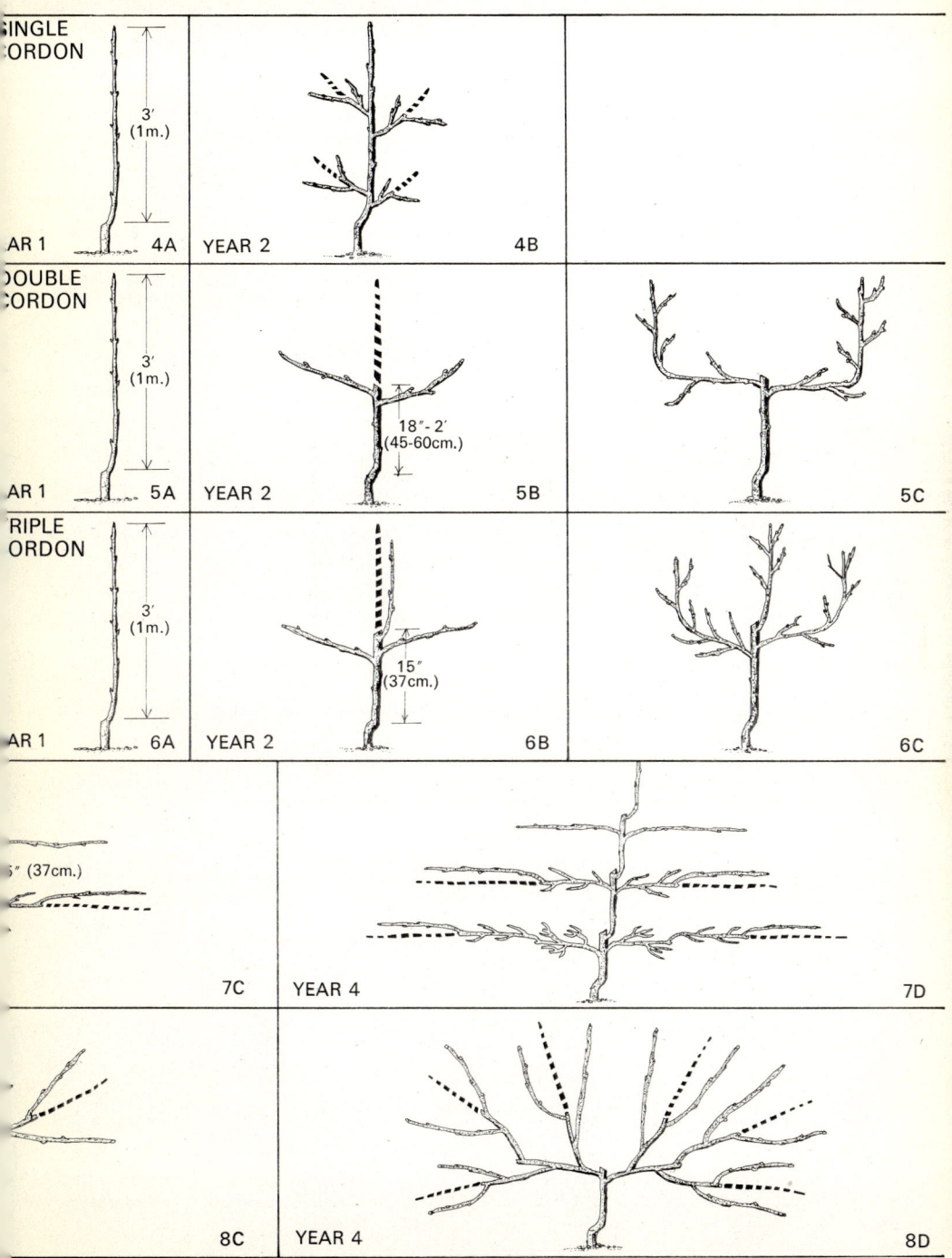

SINGLE CORDON

3' (1m.)

YEAR 1   4A

YEAR 2   4B

DOUBLE CORDON

3' (1m.)

YEAR 1   5A

YEAR 2   18" - 2' (45-60cm.)   5B

5C

TRIPLE CORDON

3' (1m.)

YEAR 1   6A

YEAR 2   15" (37cm.)   6B

6C

5" (37cm.)

7C

YEAR 4   7D

8C

YEAR 4   8D

11

Pruning for Fruit

Once the basic framework of the fruit tree has been established by winter pruning, there are several systems to follow for annual routine pruning, each system suited to certain fruits and tree shapes.

The one rule to remember is, the harder you prune the stronger will be the subsequent growth. It is of little use cutting a plant which has grown too large hard back because strong new growth will swiftly follow.

Where plants make all growth and little or no fruit it is better to tie strong growing shoots over in a half circle rather than cutting them off. Tying in an arch reduces the sap flow and encourages fruit buds to form. Another method, rather more drastic, is to dig a trench round the plant a few feet out from the stem and cut through the roots. It is suggested one half circle each side of the tree is done in a season, the tree firmly staked to prevent it blowing over in strong wind.

Fruiting on current year's growth

Grapes and *autumn fruiting* raspberries fruit on the wood made in the year of fruiting and hard pruning every winter/early spring is needed to produce strong new fruit carrying stems.

GRAPES
Single rod training under cold glass

AUTUMN

fig 8.

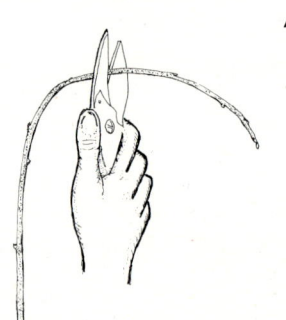

fig 9.

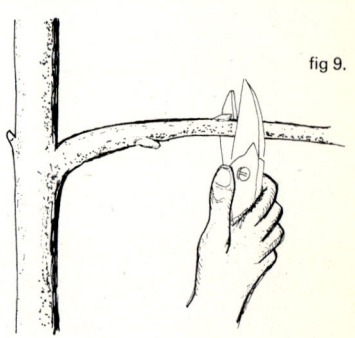

After leaf fall cut back new growth on main shoot by $\frac{1}{2}$–$\frac{1}{3}$.

Prune all side shoots back to 2 buds.

> IMPORTANT. Untie rod in winter and lower horizontally this encourages growth of side shoots.

SPRING AND SUMMER

fig 10.

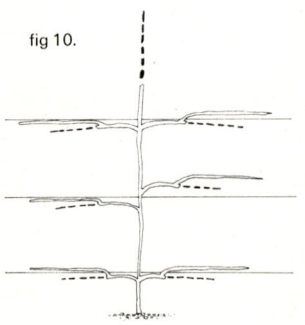

fig 11.

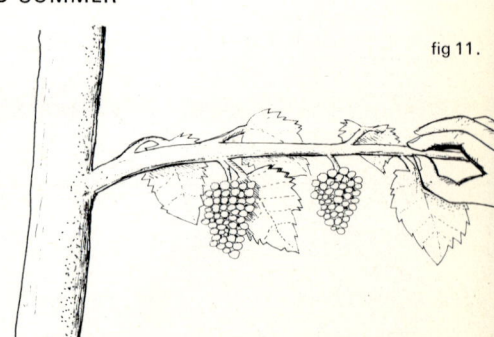

When growth recommences re-tie rod to wires. Select one good shoot from each cut back side shoot.

Tie each selected side shoot to wire when 12" long. Pinch out tip of shoot 2 leaves past flower truss.

fig 12.

pinch out shoot here

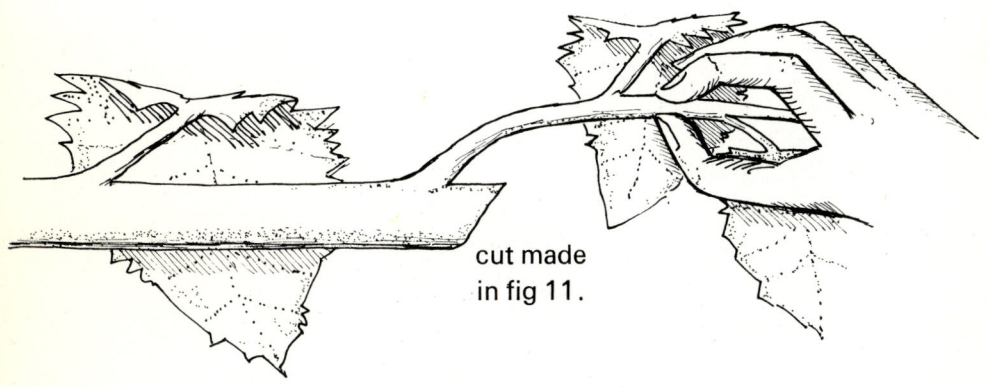

cut made
in fig 11.

If growth from pinched lateral is excessive pinch
out the second side shoot after one leaf.

Fruiting on one-year-old growth

Blackberries, blackcurrants, blueberries, cooking cherries, loganberries, nectarines, peaches and ordinary *summer fruiting* raspberries produce fruit on the previous year's growth. Excepting bush peaches and sour cherries, all these are best pruned hard back after fruiting, in other words cut out all the branches which have just borne fruit in autumn or winter to leave space for the current season's growth to carry next year's fruit and for new branches to fruit in two season's time.

An established plant. The old, dark-coloured wood is removed, leaving the new lighter-coloured wood...

Fruiting on one year, two year and older wood.

Apples, pears, gooseberries and redcurrants fruit on wood of various ages with varietal variation, for example 'Egremont Russet' apple will fruit on one year old wood. All fruit on short spurs which are from two to many years old. Before pruning established apples and pears it is important to be able to distinguish between fruit buds – plump rounded buds which develop to produce flower trusses and then fruit – and growth buds – thinner, longer, sharper buds which produce new shoots and not flowers.

Fruit bud

When prunning a branch start from the growing tip and the current year's lead shoot.

(A)

Current year's lead shoot is cut back by one half to two thirds – this produces short strong well furnished branches.

If you look back down the specimen branch it will be seen that the leader was not pruned the previous year resulting in a length of bare, unproductive branch (A). Where space is limited and old trees need rejuvenating it is worth cutting back into this older wood to encourage new growth.

14

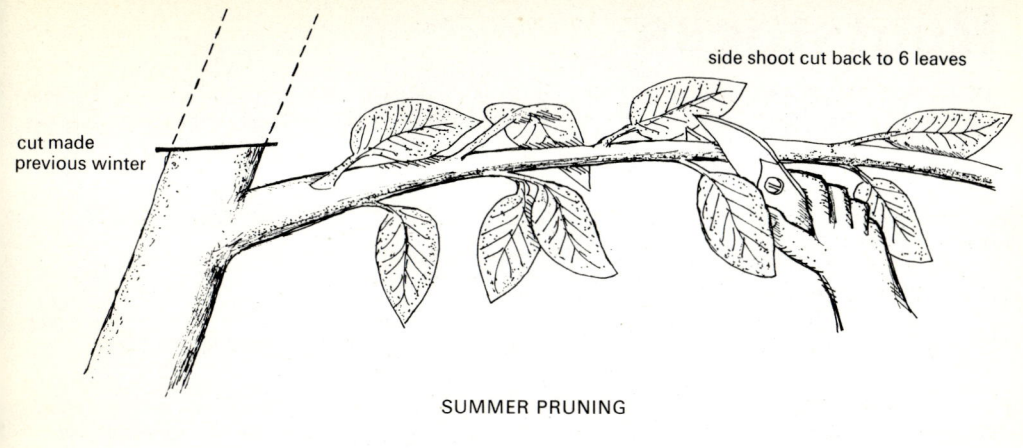

side shoot cut back to 6 leaves

cut made
previous winter

SUMMER PRUNING

SPUR PRUNING

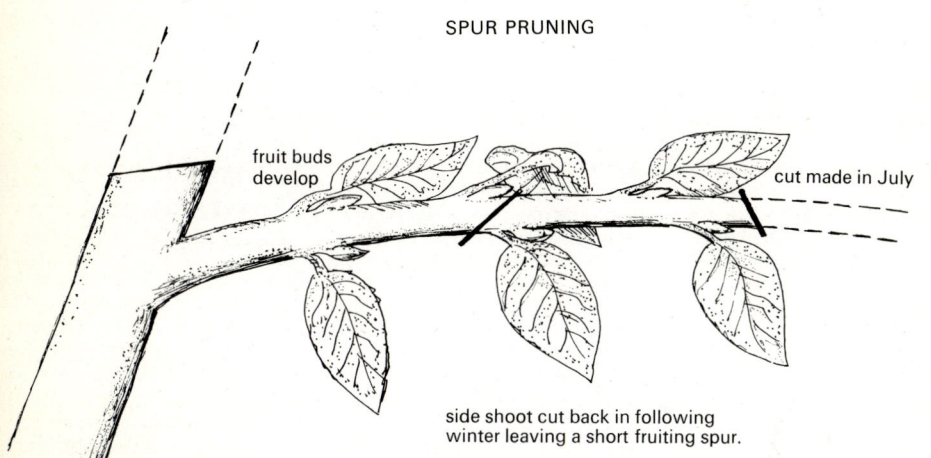

fruit buds
develop

cut made in July

side shoot cut back in following
winter leaving a short fruiting spur.

Side shoots growing from the branch are short-ened back to 6 leaves or so in July – this is called summer pruning.

This encourages the development of fruit buds and in winter these side shoots are pruned hard back to short fruiting spurs. This is called spur pruning and is used for all cordons.

Another pruning system called 'renewal' includes the summer pruning but where a number of fruit buds are produced on the shoot with 6 or so leaves it is left to fruit (*not* pruned back to a short spur).

After fruiting the shoot is pruned back hard in winter – it will then produce another side shoot to be summer pruned to develop a renewal of fruit buds. A combination of spur and renewal pruning is often best for garden bush apples.

Fruiting on one year old and older wood.

Damsons, gages, plums and sweet cherries require no pruning once the framework is estab-lished save the cutting out of diseased, dead and crossing branches immediately after fruiting. Pruning at this time reduces the chance of silver leaf infection and the diseased and dead branches are more easily seen while the tree is in leaf. Paint over the cuts after pruning.

When cutting back large neglected cherries avoid leaving horizontal wounds of 3 in. diameter and more. Wood as old as this is unlikely to produce new shoots, the wound takes a long time to callus over and the centre of the cut easily goes rotten, the rot spreading back down the middle of the branch.

Rootstocks

All the stone fruits (apricots, cherries, peaches, plums etc.) apples and pears are better grafted onto special roots rather than produced as plants on their own roots. Rootstocks, plants with special qualities in respect of root growth, have been selected and bred over the years and the significant factor in gardens is the quality of earlier fruiting and smaller trees. There are other factors such as disease resistance with certain cherry and grape stocks, pest resistance we have in some apple stocks, but size of tree and early fruiting are our prime consideration. We must wait until 1979–80 before we have the new dwarfing stock Colt for cherries, a stock which could revolutionise cherry growing. We also await really dwarfing stocks for plums and gages but have a choice for apples, thanks to the work undertaken at East Malling and Long Ashton Research Stations

Apple Rootstocks

M9 (Malling 9) the most dwarfing stock and suitable for gardens where soil conditions are good and the gardener maintains a high standard of cultivation. It is essential to keep trees on this stock *securely staked* for the *whole* of *their life.*

M 26 (Malling 26) recently introduced and slightly stronger growing than M 9, this stock will need secure staking in poor sandy soils. Likely to start fruiting very early, that is in the second and third year from grafting.
The above two varieties are ideal for cordons, dwarf pyramid and bush apples.

M 7 (Malling 7) is the next up in strength of growth but being replaced by the more recent *MM106* (Malling Merton 106) Both are described as semi-dwarfing because on good soils they provide medium sized trees and on poor soils dwarf trees. MM 106 is recommended as the best allround stock for gardens.

M 2 (Malling 2) was used extensively commercially but is now succeeded by *MM 111* (Malling Merton 111). Both are vigorous rootstocks producing excellent bush trees, MM 111 is resistant to drought conditions and is best for really poor soils. Trees on these two stocks will come into fruit several years later than the dwarfing ones but will give heavier yields. Suitable stocks for bush and standard trees.

Pear Rootstocks

EM Quince A (East Malling Quince A) is the stock recommended for general garden use. *EM Quince C* has more dwarfing effect but needs to be used with a vigorous growing variety and on good soils.
EM Quince A produces trees 12 feet (3.6m.) in diameter.

Stone Fruit Rootstocks

other than cherries.

St. Julien 'A' is the most dwarfing stock and best suited to the small garden. *Brompton* is more vigorous and the one to use where heavy cropping varieties are grown well.
St. Julien produces trees 12–15 ft. diameter (3.6–4.6m.).
Brompton produces trees 18–20 ft. diameter (5.5–5.8m.).

Rough guide to diameter of bush trees in a range of varieties on various stocks

	Bramley (strong growing)	Discovery (medium)	Cox's O.P. (least vigorous)
M9	16 ft. (5 m.)	12 ft. (3.6 m.)	10 ft. (3 m.)
M26	20 ft. (6.1 m.)	15 ft. (4.6 m.)	11 ft. (3.3 m.)
MM106	25 ft. (7.5 m.)	16 ft. (5 m.)	12 ft. (3.6 m.)
MM111	30 ft. (9 m.)	20 ft. (5.8 m.)	15 ft. (4.6 m.)

These figures provide a guide to planting distances between trees on the various stocks.

Fruit selection

Apricots

The most popular variety grown in Britain today is Apricot 'Moorpark', it is said to have been raised in Hertfordshire way back in 1760.

How to Grow

Just as easy as plum, although flowering in March they must receive protection from frost. In very mild areas, they can be planted in the open garden. South of Birmingham fruit may be produced on trees planted against south facing walls and fences, given some netting once the flower buds show colour, to provide frost protection. Elsewhere, grow under glass which can be freely ventilated in summer.

Apricots are self pollinating, help this by hand pollinating, — dust over the open flowers with a feather at midday in sunny weather. General fertiliser, up to 2 oz. per square yard, can be worked into the surface in spring. A mulch of manure or well rotted compost helps retain moisture. Be sure the trees do nor dry out during the period April to June.

Prune

Fruit is produced on spurs as well as on branches produced the previous year. This means less pruning than on other fan trained stone fruit once established. Prune back the lead shoots to each main branch to 15 inches (38 cm.) in August. All side shoots are stopped by pinching out the growing tip when about 3 in. (8 cm.) long, and subsequent growth stopped after one leaf. This helps to develop fruiting spurs. Tie in lead shoots and additional branches while they are still young and supple.

Harvest

Mid August outside.

Propagate

Apricots are grafted or budded on plum root stocks, 'St. Julien A' a semi dwarfing stock is best.

Pests and Diseases

Under glass in hot dry conditions the tiny red spider mite attacks the leaves turning them yellowy bronze rather than green. Syringe with water to increase humidity and spray with Malathion or derris.
Sudden 'die-back' of branches is caused by fungus entering wounds. Avoid making large pruning cuts and cover any cut woody surfaces.

Notes

Try growing apricots in large tubs to flower under cold glass and then stand out in summer to ripen.

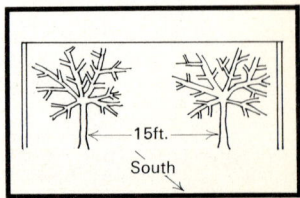

15ft.

South

Apples

Introduction

Smaller gardens are no case for eliminating apples, every garden needs some form of tree and a bush apple on the right stock will remain an acceptable size. Further, it provides attractive blossom in spring, pea sticks from the annual pruning and eventually logs, after years of providing fruit fresh from the tree.

While bush trees are the most popular look for specimens which have a trunk a little taller than usual, sometimes called 'bush-on-a-leg'. Shorter than half standards, they do not get too high for picking but have sufficient clear stem to make mowing and cultivating beneath the branches easy.

Cross pollination of different apple varieties is necessary for regular heavy crops. Select varieties which flower at a similar time (see selector chart). Apple trees in neighbours' gardens will supply the cross pollination and remember the flowering crab — 'Golden Hornet' — is a very good pollinator and its decorative yellow fruits can also be used for crab apple jelly.

How to Grow

All well cultivated garden soils are suitable for apples. The more demanding varieties like Cox's Orange Pippin are better avoided in northern districts and on poor soils. When planting see that the graft, the knobbly section of stem above soil level, is clear of the soil. If you cover the graft with soil the variety will produce its own roots and the effects of root-stock will be lost.

Where the graft has been made well above the soil line, planting several inches deeper — without covering the graft — reduces the staking requirement and en-

Arthur Turner

'**Arthur Turner**' (illustrated with blossom) is a cooking apple to grow for its attractive flowers and greenish-yellow fruit August—October. Crops well in all parts of the country and forms an upright tree.

'**Blenheim Orange**' makes a large tree, slow to fruit, big eating apples orange-yellow, good flavour, November- February, can be cooked.

'**Bramley's Seedling**' makes a very large tree, wide spreading branches, cooking apple November-February. Last two varieties do not provide pollen to cross other varieties and are not recommended for small gardens but both fruits can be frozen.

courages earlier and heavier fruiting. Avoid planting in hollows where cold spring frosts form and choose late flowering varieties for such gardens.

Pruning

Apples can be either spur or renewal pruned although with compact growing varieties like C. Ross, Discovery, Epicure, Egremont, Fortune, Grenadier, J. Grieve, L. Derby, Ellison, Wilks and Worcester bush trees will crop regularly without pruning once the initial branch framework has been estab-lished. All trees are best with the lead shoots of the current year's growth pruned back by half each year. Cordon and espalier trained trees should be spur pruned.

Pruning is one of the best methods of disease control, all shoots showing signs of mil-dew in early summer, for example, are best pruned out and burnt before they have a chance to spread.

Harvesting

Take care when picking fruit, snatching apples from the tree can break off the spur and remove next year's fruit bud. Hold the apple and lift up through 90° from the branch and if the apple is ready to pick it will come away easily.

Where trees either produce too many small fruit or fruit heavily every other year, with no fruit in the year between, thin out in early July, leaving one apple every 6–9 in. down the branch, wider spacing for bigger apples. Apples are stored in trays in a cool slightly damp atmosphere. Remove fruit once ripe or it will speed ripening of adjacent apples.

Charles Ross

'**Charles Ross**' (illus-trated) large very attractive fruit October–December. Compact tree with disease resistant leaves, grows well in all parts of the country. Eating Apple.

'**Cox's Orange Pippin**' (Queen Cox – the red fruit form illustrated). Superb flavour October–December, this eating apple re-quires good soil and warm climate. Susceptible to disease.

'**Discovery**' (illus.) rec-ently introduced, this is an excellent early apple. Delicious, juicy fruit, esp-ecially when picked ripe from the tree. Successful in all parts of the country with disease resistant foliage.

Cox's Orange Pippin

Discovery

Pests and Diseases

Listed here are the more common pests and diseases and cultural — rather than chemical (see pages 60–62) ways of reducing attack. Reasonable crops can be grown without spraying, look out for trouble and early action will reduce the need to spray.

Birds take ripe fruit and in winter bullfinches peck off the dormant buds. Netting gives protection.

Aphis (greenfly etc.) cause the leaves to curl, distort shoots and feel sticky. Tar oil winter wash and pruning off distorted twigs with overwintering eggs gives the trees a clean start.

Woolly aphis — well named with waxy white covering protecting the aphis require forceful spring sprays to control.

Caterpillars of winter and tortrix moth, eating leaves in spring, catch the adults by applying a band of grease round the trunk October to March.

Maggots which have entered the fruit in one neat hole are from *codlin moth*, this pest and *apple blossom weevil* are trapped by wrapping either sacking or corrugated cardboard around the tree in June. Remove and burn in October, see that bark under wrap is cut down fairly smooth.

Maggots which eat the surface of fruit before burrowing in come from *sawfly*, the fruits drop before they ripen. Pick up and destroy fallen fruit in June to reduce chance of attack next year.

Canker causes discoloured hollows in the bark which gradually get larger, the wood around swells and if girdled the piece of branch above dies. Cut out diseased areas, burn chips and paint wound.

Mildew causes greyish growth over shoots and leaves, first

21

Egremont Russet

seen in early spring as young growth starts. Cut out infected shoots as soon as they appear and keep the trees well watered in dry summer weather to reduce chance of this disease spreading.

Scab causes brown and blackish spots on the leaves and fruits. Light green patches also develop on the leaves. Rake up and burn all fallen leaves, especially those which fall prematurely.

TIP: Keep soil around newly planted trees weed-free. Competition from weeds in the first year can reduce growth by 50%, an effect continued well into the tree's life. Weed competition is likely to do most damage May/June.

Grenadier

'Egremont Russet' (illus.) neat upright growth flowering and fruiting very early in the tree's life. The best russet with characteristic flavour October-December. Suitable for all parts of the country and resistant to disease. Excellent for small gardens.

'Ellison's Orange' with a red fruited form 'Red Ellison', distinctive flavour and delicious eaten ripe from the tree. Flowers resistant to frost.

Laxton's **'Epicure'** a pretty striped fruit, excellent flavour on small tree. Disease resistant and suitable for all parts of the country.

Golden Delicious

James Grieve

Laxton's **'Fortune'** crops from an early age, fruit striped red on yellow, delicious flavour September–October. Suitable for all parts of the country and disease resistant.

'Grenadier' (illus.) the best early cooking apple usually picked green but turning yellow as it ripens. Just a little later than 'Early Victoria' (also called Emneth Early) and all three known as "codlin apples". 'Grenadier' is suitable for all parts of the country, is free cropping and disease resistant.

'Golden Delicious' (illus.) resistant to frost and easy to grow. So freely available in fruit shops that gardeners usually select varieties with better flavour.

'Idared' a valuable cooking apple because it cooks well from November to March. A little sharp flavoured but can be eaten February/May. Susceptible to mildew and a watch should be kept for this disease.

'James Grieve' (illus.) perhaps the best of all garden apples, easy to grow, regular heavy crops with apples which can be picked early to cook and eaten fresh from the tree when ripe. The fruit bruises easily and does not travel well.

Lord Derby

Spartan

'**Lord Derby**' (illus.) large cooking apple October—December turns reddish when cooked. Easy to grow in all parts of the country, upright and disease resistant.

'**Merton Knave**' recently introduced early eating apple, bright red sweet flavour and crisp August/September. Suitable all parts of the country.

'**Rev. W. Wilks**' large cooking apple pale yellow when ripe September/November. Suitable for the small garden and easy to grow. Disease resistant.

'**Spartan**' (illus.) dessert apple November/January with characteristic colour. Flowers resistant to spring frost, disease resistant and suited to the small garden.

'**Worcester Pearmain**' attractive flowers and fruit, easy to grow and best eaten ripe from the tree. Suitable for all districts and small gardens. Disease resistant.

(Planting distance — see root-stocks on page 16).

Apple Selector Chart

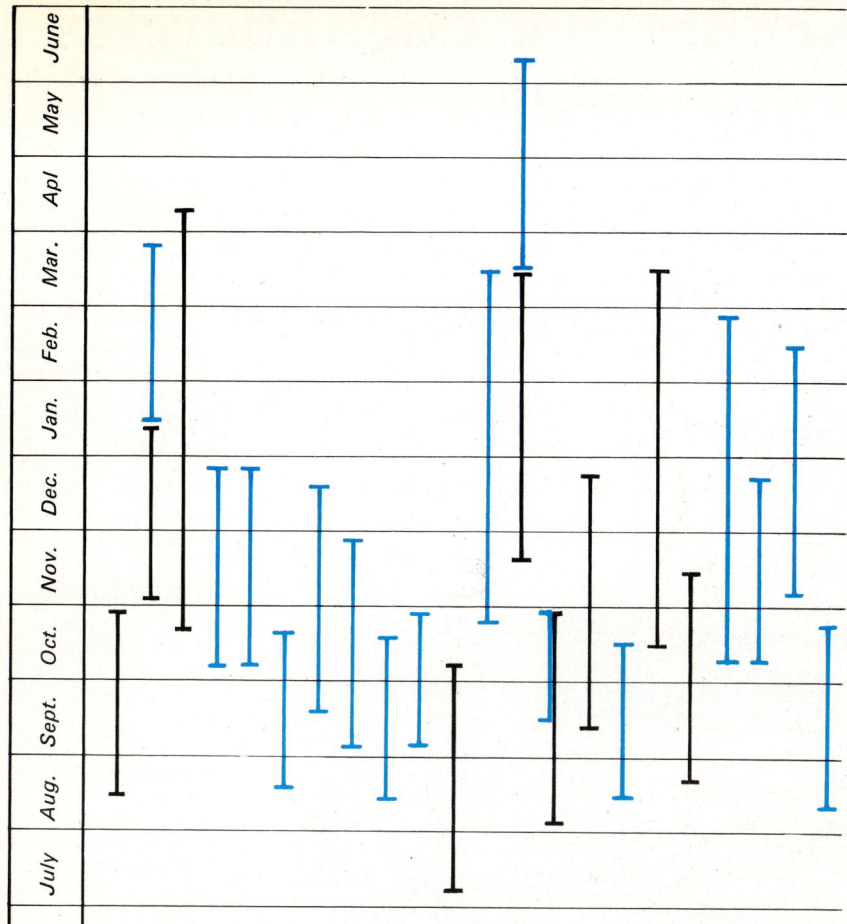

	July	Aug.	Sept.	Oct.	Nov.	Dec.	Jan.	Feb.	Mar.	Apl	May	June

(M) 'ARTHUR TURNER' *
(M) 'BLENHEIM ORANGE' (T)
(M) 'BRAMLEY'S SEEDLING' (T)
(M) 'CHARLES ROSS' *
(M) 'COX'S ORANGE PIPPIN'
(E) 'DISCOVERY' *
(E) 'EGREMONT RUSSET' *
(L) 'ELLISON'S ORANGE'
(M) 'EPICURE' (LAXTON'S)
(M) 'FORTUNE' (LAXTON'S)
(M) 'GRENADIER' *
(L) 'GOLDEN DELICIOUS'
(E) 'IDARED'
(M) 'JAMES GRIEVE' *
(L) 'LORD DERBY' *
(M) 'MERTON KNAVE'
(L) 'NEWTON WONDER'
(M) 'REV. W. WILKS' *
(L) 'SPARTAN'
(M) 'SUNSET' (LAXTON'S) . .
(L) 'SUPERB' (LAXTON'S)
(M) 'WORCESTER PEARMAIN' *

* = Good Garden Varieties in all parts of the country

Cooking ▬▬ Dessert ▬▬

The Flowering time is indicated E — Early, M — Mid-season, L — Late. Choose two varieties with similar flowering time for cross pollination or plant one Flowering Crab Golden Hornet.
T — Triploid. These trees do not provide viable pollen so plant three varieties including the Triploid.

Blackberries, Loganberries
and Hybrid Berries

Grouped with blackberries are loganberries, thought by some people to be a cross between blackberry and red raspberry, and other hybrids, the results of crosses between blackberries, loganberries and raspberries. All require similar cultural treatment and all are excellent fruits for deep freezing.

Blackberries

Some people may think the hedgerow a better place for blackberries than the garden but they could not be further from the truth. Named varieties

of blackberry are adaptable to virtually all gardens and garden situations, they crop freely over a long period and have the advantage of big berries and luscious flavour. The best hedgerow blackberries may well be on the top of the hedge but cultivated berries will all be within easy reach.

Varieties

'Bedford Giant' – an early, late July to late August, and large fruiting kind, sweet fruits on plants of medium vigour and prickly.
'Himalaya Giant' – fruits from

mid August to October, rather sharp in flavour and very strong growing. This prickly variety will yield over 20 lb. of fruit from a single plant.
'Oregon Thornless' – also called 'Evergreen Thornless', fruits from early September to October, huge succulent berries with delicious bramble flavour. Attractive cut leaves, also called 'Parsley-type' leaves, are attractive and virtually evergreen. Of medium vigour and needs plenty of water to get maximum berry size. One plant will yield over 10 lb.

How to Grow

Ideal to train against a shed, wall, fence or stretch of wires between stout posts. Shaded sites and north facing walls are acceptable, they are slightly lower yielding, however, than more open and sunny sites. All soils are suitable and the biggest, juiciest fruits will come from good soil to which manure and compost has been added. Remember, these fruits will crop for 12–15 years so prepare the soil well before planting. Plant the more vigorous varieties on poor soil, the thornless kinds being invariably less vigorous than the thorned. All are self pollinating and, flowering in July, frost is no problem. Avoid digging around the roots, it is much better to lightly hoe the surface to control weeds and mulch each spring with well rotted compost.

Prune

After fruiting cut out at ground level all the stems which have borne fruit. Tie up the new stems as they develop keeping them away from fruiting stems. Once the fruited stems have been pruned out bring down

Blackberry "Oregon Thornless"
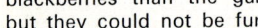

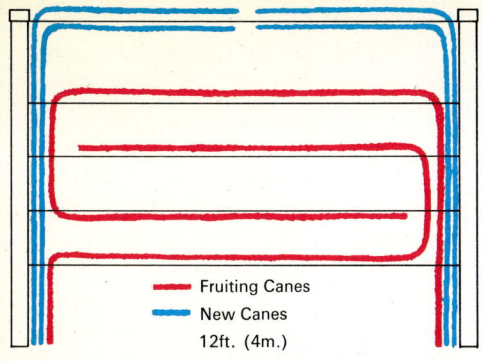
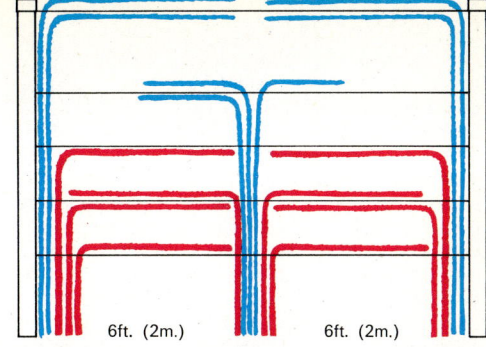

Fruiting Canes
New Canes
12ft. (4m.)

6ft. (2m.)   6ft. (2m.)

and tie in the new branches for next season's crop. Four methods of training are shown in the plant spacing diagrams. Use the closer spacing, 6 ft. (2 m.) apart for the less vigorous varieties and plants on poor soil.

Container and pot grown plants will fruit the summer following planting. Bare root plants are transplanted October to March and cut back to 9 in. (23 cm.) above the soil. It may take two seasons for good fruit carrying stems to be produced with bare root plants transplanted in spring.

Blackberry

Harvest

From late July to late October according to variety. Where the stems are tied in regularly to wires and similar supports, 2, 3, 4 and 5 feet from the ground picking and plant control is easy.

Propagation

The tips of young shoots root quite quickly in July/August. Bend a healthy shoot tip and hold it down in 6 in. (15 cm.) of well cultivated soil, either with a piece of wire bent staple-shape or a heavy stone. Sever from the parent plant in October leaving 12 in. (30 cm.) of stem. The following spring these rooted tips can be transplanted in their fruiting position.

Pests

Greenfly and other aphis can be troublesome and are controlled by spraying with Malathion. The same chemical sprayed when most of the petals have fallen will control the raspberry beetle which causes the small maggots in fruit.

Notes

A firm support of posts and galvanised wire or wires fixed through wire eyes to walls and fences is essential to keep vigorous brambles 'tied down'.

27

Loganberry

The original loganberry was raised from seed in Judge J. H. Logan's garden at Santa Cruz, California in 1881. Later the thornless form came from the same state and even more recently at the East Malling Research Station in Kent special plants — what the nurserymen call selected clones — have been selected and freed from virus disease. These selected clones are sold under number.

Varieties

LOGANBERRY 'LY 59', a very heavy cropping plant which produces thorned canes 8 feet long bearing long, dark fruits.
LOGANBERRY 'LY 654', the best thornless strain which is easier to train and not so vigorous. Large burgundy red fruits up to 2 in. long are borne in profusion.

How to Grow

Nearly all soils and sites are suitable, slightly acid soil conditions are thought best so do not lime and add extra well rotted compost and manure to chalky soils. The loganberry requires a slightly warmer site than blackberry. Organic matter, that is well rotted compost, is also needed on heavy soils to improve drainage and on sandy soils to retain moisture in summer.
Keep the plants well watered once fruits have set to get the largest berries.

Prune

As for blackberries.

Loganberry

Harvest

In July and August once the fruit is ripe hold between thumb and first two fingers and gently twist from the stem. Let the fruit roll into the palm of the hand and several fruits can be picked before emptying into the bowl.

Propagate

As for blackberries.

Pests

The small reddish maggot of raspberry beetle. Spray with derris or malathion about the second and last weeks of June, avoid spraying plants in flower.

Diseases

Cane spot causes circular purple spots on the stems, leaves and flower stalks in May and June. The spots get larger and the centres turn grey. Cut out diseased stems and spray with copper fungicide before flowering and once fruit has set. Keeping the new canes tied above the fruiting ones and pruning as soon as possible reduces the risk of disease spreading from one year to the next. This disease is more likely in wet seasons.
Spur Blight, dark purple blotches which turn silver grey where leaf joins the stem. Spray emerging canes with benlate and then two or three successive sprays at 10–14 day intervals.

Hybrids

'BOYSENBERRY' is said to be a mixture of blackberry, loganberry and raspberry. It has large dark red to black fruit with sharp and distinct flavour.
'THORNLESS BOYSENBERRY' raised in California in the 1930's and now available in Britain. The fruit is red in July but ripens to purplish black in August. It has a good flavour and small pips, one plant will yield 8 lb. of fruit.

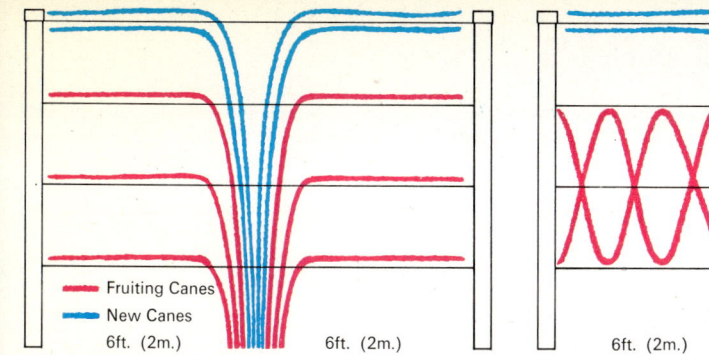
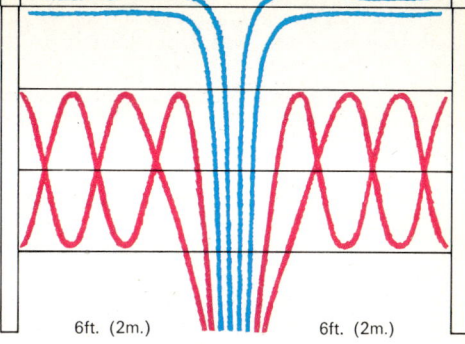

Fruiting Canes
New Canes
6ft. (2m.)　　6ft. (2m.)　　　6ft. (2m.)　　6ft. (2m.)

'JAPANESE WINEBERRY' has light fresh green leaves and contrasting crimson hairs up the stem with a scattering of sharp thorns. Almost self supporting and a useful plant for the larger shrub border. After flowering the calyx folds around the developing fruit to unfold later to expose amber yellow turning to wine red fruits in August. The whole truss ripens at once and can be cut to serve on the stem. It follows the summer fruiting raspberry and is an attractive and interesting plant.

'YOUNGBERRY' very similar to the 'Boysenberry' and seldom listed.

Thornless Boysenberry

How to Grow

These hybrids are more drought resistant and will survive on light sandy soils. Moisture is needed in July/August when the berries swell, however, to obtain the largest fruit. Where several rows of blackberries and hybrid berries are grown across the garden, allow 6 feet between the rows. Closer spacing in the row for Japanese Wineberry and the less vigorous thornless types.

Prune

As for blackberries.

Harvest

Gather when ripe and dry, wet fruit will soon develop moulds unless eaten or cooked immediately.

Propagation

As for blackberries, the Japanese Wineberry can also be propagated from semi-hardwood cuttings 4–6 in. long taken in August and September from the current season's growth.

Disease

Grey mould on the fruit of all black and hybrid berries can be controlled by spraying with benlate. This disease is usually only a problem in very wet seasons. Spray just as the flowers open and then twice more at 10–14 day intervals.

Blackcurrants

Very high in Vitamin C and one of the most popular soft fruits for jams, tarts, fruit juice and flavouring for ice cream, this bush is easy to grow and a must for the smallest garden.

Varieties

'Amos Black' is late with small upright branches, 'Baldwin' is a popular late variety making a compact bush on heavy soil, 'Boskoop Giant', one of the earliest to ripen with very large fruits on each string — the early ones need picking separately — a good variety for exhibition. 'Wellington XXX', a good all round garden variety. Watch for the new 'Tenah' which has given up to double the yield of older varieties like 'Amos Black' but grows into a larger bush.

How to Grow

All garden soils are suitable and if they are moisture retaining and yet free draining, so much the better. Late frost damages the flowers and cold, wet and windy conditions discourage pollination, both reduce cropping. A sheltered site and choice of a late variety help to avoid this.

Plant 4–6 feet (1.2–2 m) apart, the closer spacing in the row, the wider spacing between rows, in October to March for bare root plants, container plants any time.

It will be difficult to overfeed this plant, apply manure or well rotted compost as a mulch each spring and 3–4 ounces Growmore per square yard (m²). Try to avoid digging around the bushes, control weeds by mulching to get the heaviest crop.

Prune

After planting bare root bushes cut them down to within 1–2 inches (2–5 cm) of the soil. This ensures strong establishment and new branches to fruit in the second year. After the first summer and immediately for container grown plants, cut the weakest shoots out to encourage new growth for the following season. The remaining shoots will bear fruit the following summer.

Once established and fruiting cut out old fruited wood every winter, always choose the oldest wood — it is very black in colour. Where big bushes have old branches with four or more young laterals cut back to one lateral to encourage more new growth from the base. The bigger the bush and the more young one-year-old light coloured branches, the heavier the crop is likely to be.

Harvest

Over ten years the average bush is likely to yield 6–8 lb per bush per year in July, the late varieties just into August in the north. Pick dry and when the fruit is black but still firm.

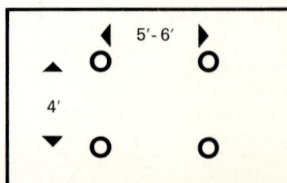

Propagation

Cuttings 8–10 inches (25 cm) long of the current year's growth are taken from *disease free* bushes in October/early November and pushed 6–8 inches (15–18 cm) into the soil. They root very easily.

Pests and Diseases

Big Bud Mite – a very descriptive name because infected buds swell up several times larger than normal and are easily seen in winter – spreads virus diseases which reduce yield.

While lime sulphur sprayed when leaves are the size of a 5p piece (March/April) will control this pest, destruction and replanting with new 'certified' disease-free plants is best in the long term.

Red and White Currants

The white currants are not widely grown but are very much like small white grapes, delicious eaten fresh as a dessert. Red currants, on the other hand, have many uses, being eaten as jelly with meat, used with other fruits like raspberries in pies, tarts and puddings as well as in jams and preserves. Both red and white currants need the same cultural conditions.

Varieties

All will do well. 'Red Lake' has large fruit on long trusses and recently introduced red varieties like the very early and vigorous growing 'Jonkheer van Tets' and the late 'Rondom' are heavy yielding.

How to Grow

A little more demanding than blackcurrants, they are best in lighter, free draining soils, not too chalky and protected from strong wind. Plant 4–5 feet (1.2–1.5 m) apart, the wider spacing for more vigorous varieties, from October to March for bare root bushes, anytime for container grown plants.

Mix plenty of well rotted compost into the soil before planting and mulch each spring to help retain moisture. Add a general fertiliser high in potash – for example a rose or tomato fertiliser – each spring at 1½–2 ounces (43–57 gm) per square yard.

Bushes on a 9–12 inch (23–30cm) stem are the easiest to grow but where space is limited red and white currants can be trained as single, double and triple stemmed cordons against a fence and on a 2–3 feet high stem as standards.

Prune

Just the same as apple trees. Young bushes which have grown for two summers have the current year's main branch tips cut back by half and the side shoots on young and established plants cut back to 1 in. (2.5 cm.) to form fruiting spurs. Established plants can have the occasional old branch cut out completely and replaced by new growth. Once branches have reached the required height each season's new lead growth can be cut back to 1 in. (2.5 cm.). Aim for 6–8 good branches.

Where bushes make excessive growth and little fruit, cut back all the side shoots to leave them 5–6 leaves long in July, then prune again to 1 in. (2.5 cm.) in winter.

Propagate

Cuttings from the current year's growth are taken October/November 12 in. (30 cm.) long and all buds removed except the top three or four. This gives the clear stem to keep fruit up away from soil splashes and makes picking easier. See Gooseberry for cordon training. Standards are trained as for apples.

Harvest

An average of 4–5 lb. from each established bush in July.

Pests

Net to protect from birds in winter and summer and spray to control greenfly which pucker the leaves and cause reddish leaf blisters.

Disease

Red spots on the wood are caused by coral spot. Prune back to disease-free wood and cover cut with grafting or pruning paste.

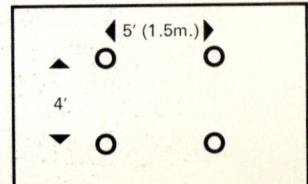

How to plant a bush

Protect from drying winds.

Dig hole large enough to accommodate outstretched roots.

Fill in with peat and soil, covering the base of the bush and prune back after planting.

How to plant a tree

Dig hole large enough to accommodate outstretched roots and to the depth of soil mark on the trunk.

A cane placed across the top of the hole allows check on planting depth. See the graft point indicated is well above the soil.

Mix peat in the base of the hole and drive stake in firmly before repositioning tree.

Firm around the roots with soil and peat while filling in.

Secure head of tree to top of stake with a tree tie and prune branches in early spring.

An alternative method of staking, suitable for container grown trees, is to drive the stake at 45°, top of stake facing into the wind.

Cherries

Sweet cherries eaten fresh require different cultural treatments to the sour or culinary varieties used for jam, bottling and tarts.

Cooking or Acid Cherries

Easy to grow given well cultivated soil and especially suitable for the smaller garden as bush and for trained specimens. The variety 'Morello' is the best known, self fertile, quick to fruit and strongly recommended. It grows well as a fan trained tree even against a north facing fence or wall. The fruit can be gathered in August when dark red but if left becomes almost black in September. 'Kentish Red' grows larger and requires 'Morello' as pollinator.

Add plenty of well rotted compost to the soil before planting to ensure the trees do not lack moisture in summer. Mulch in early spring to retain moisture, especially fan trained trees against walls. The now standard vigorous cherry rootstock Prunus avium is suitable for 'Morello' which is naturally dwarf in habit and tends to be weak growing.

Prune

All fruit is borne on the previous year's growth so unpruned bush trees have all the fruit carried on the outer circumference. Trees should be rejuvenated by cutting the occasional branch back into three— and four-year old wood to produce strong new fruiting branches. Fan trained trees are pruned the same as peaches. Prune early spring when growth buds are more easily seen and wounds heal more quickly to reduce chance of silver leaf disease entry.

Harvest

It is best to gather by cutting off with scissors, if fruits are pulled off there is the chance of tearing away a piece of bark and the risk of infection of the branch by brown rot.

Pests (ACID AND SWEET)

All cherries will need protection from birds by nets or black cotton stretched over the branches.
Aphis (blackfly) can be a real pest and the recommended aphis sprays will be necessary to prevent shoot distortion.

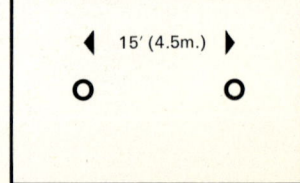

15' (4.5m.)

Sweet Cherries

There are a number of succulent dessert varieties but on the ordinary stocks they grow too large for the small garden and to make matters worse they are impossible to protect from birds, take a number of years to fruit and need two varieties to cross pollinate and set fruit. We must wait until 1980 for the new dwarfing stock Colt (E. M. Fb 2/58 No. 21 — thank goodness for the name Colt!) which will bring sweet cherries into the small garden.

Sweet cherries require good deep soils, they are more demanding in this respect than acid kinds. Best results will be achieved in warm and sheltered spots in the garden.

Propagate

Most sweet cherries will not set fruit with their own pollen and many will not cross pollinate with one another. To avoid complication either seek the nurseryman's advice when purchasing trees or select 'Merton Glory' an early white fleshed fruit and 'Van' a late variety with dark red flesh. 'Morello' will provide pollen to pollinate both these varieties but tends to flower too late. 'Van' cross pollinates with 'Merton Glory' which fruits early in its life and pollinates most varieties. Watch out for 'Stella', a self pollin-ating dessert cherry.

Prune

Large wall area — over 8 ft. (2·41 m) high — is needed for fan trees on F12/1 stock. The lead shoots are not pruned back but either left or cut out to leave a weaker side shoot in its place, or tied down to the horizontal to check growth. Rub out all shoots growing at right angles to the wall and tie in laterals as for peaches. Other growth is pruned back at 6–8 leaves, then pruned back to 4 leaves in early autumn.

Harvest

Just gather once ripe and eat from the tree.

Diseases
(ACID OR SWEET)

Bacterial Canker causes brown spots on the leaves which fall out to leave holes. Infected branches produce small yellow leaves and die-back. Cut these out and cover the wound with protective paint.

Silver Leaf. Cut back all dead wood 6 in. (15 cm.) into clean live wood, that is 6 in. beyond brown stain seen in diseased wood, and paint over wounds.

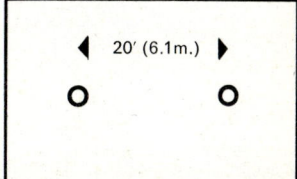

◀ 20' (6.1m.) ▶

Figs

A cold greenhouse in the north or warm, sunny south corner between fences in the south, is needed if ripe figs are to be gathered in September/October in this country. The fig grows too easily in Britain and as well as finding a warm situation some root restriction is needed in all but the poorest soils.

How to Grow

Fig 'Brown Turkey' is the variety commonly offered for sale and pot grown plants are best planted in March. A hole approximately 3 ft. (1 m.) × 2 ft. (60 cm.) is best excavated and the sides and base lined with galvanised iron, paving slabs or similar material. The base, free draining but again root restricting. Planting in a large container or half a cleaned out oil drum with drainage hole is the other alternative. Free draining soil with moisture mid summer is the ideal.

Prune

Any pruning is best done in July. Grow like bush apples with very little pruning or roughly fan train against a wall. Prune fan branches by cutting back the side shoots to 4 in. (10 cm.) early June and tie in the resulting new growth which will bear fruit at each leaf along the stem. The tiny immature fruits on the well ripened shoot tips need protecting by wrapping around with straw in winter in exposed situations and cold weather outside.

Remove the straw protection in spring and prune out any wood which has been damaged over-winter. At this time the plump buds seen at each leaf joint on the shoot ends will develop into figs.

Harvest

Fruits not much larger than a halfpenny in early autumn are best removed from outdoor plants as they are unlikely to develop. Gather fruits as the stem collapses, they colour and are soft to the touch August-October.

Pests and Diseases

None to worry about.

Tips

Liquid feed established plants with a promising crop in sunny weather, July/August for a bumper harvest.

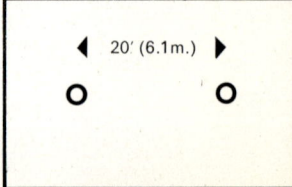

◀ 20' (6.1m.) ▶

Gooseberries

One of the earliest of bush fruits and cropping over 8–10 weeks, gooseberries are useful for many summer desserts including pies, fools and stewed. They are excellent for bottling, making jams and for freezing. The yellow varieties left to ripen on the bush are delicious fresh, and quite as succulent as large grapes.

Varieties

'Careless' is easy to grow, green, heavy cropping and mid season ripening. 'Keepsake' can be picked as early if not earlier than 'Careless' for cooking, but is late ripening and pale green. Strong growing, it makes large bushes in time and is better protected from frost in cold sites. 'Leveller' ripens to produce large succulent yellow fruits, the best dessert variety but requiring good soil to flourish. Another easy to grow variety is 'Whinham's Industry', upright growth in early years precedes more arching growth. Ripening to produce red fruits, sweet flavoured with hairy skin,

it is mid season ripening and one of the most successful in heavier soils.

How to Grow

A sunny site is best but partial shade will give acceptable yields. The more demanding varieties will do better in cold areas, given the protection of a south facing fence to protect from wind and frost in spring. Cultivation is similar to that for red and white currants, use either the better soils or garden soils improved by the addition of plenty of well rotted compost before planting. Gooseberries are generally more tolerant of chalk than other soft fruits.

A general fertiliser high in potash should be worked into the soil before planting and each spring at 1–2 oz. per square yard (28–57 gm. m²). A spring mulch of well rotted compost will smother weeds, retain moisture to increase berry size and improve growth. The mulch is best applied after flowering where spring frost is a possibility.

Plant 4–6 ft. (1.25–1.8 m.) apart, the wider distances between rows and for the more vigorous varieties likely to be cropped for up to fifteen years. Space single cordons 1 ft. (30 cm.) – double cordons 2 ft. (60 cm.) and triple cordons 3 ft. (90 cm.) apart down the row. Gooseberries are easiest to cultivate around and pick if grown on a short stem, 6–9 in. (15–22 cm.) high. It may be necessary to remove one or two roots and one or two low branches when planting to achieve this.

Prune

Much the same as redcurrants, the lead shoots are cut back by one half of the summer's growth in winter. Bullfinches can strip the buds from goose-berries in winter so either delay pruning until early spring – to give the birds more buds to go at and reduce the chance of their removing the buds we require – or net the bushes. Prune drooping branches back to an upward growing bud to get more upright branches. Once the branches have reach-ed the required height and length cut the lead shoots back to 1 in. (2.5 cm.) or so each winter.

Side shoots are pruned back to 5–6 leaves in July and cut further back to 1 in. (2.5 cm.) in winter. (see illus. page 15) Pruning these side-shoots into short fruiting spurs gives larger single fruits of better quality. Where yield rather than quality is the aim, with fruit being picked green for culinary purposes, pruning more along the lines of black-currant is recommended. Here strong new growth from the centre of the bush is encour-aged and the occasional older branch cut out to make space for the new.

Harvest

Thin the green fruits to leave one berry every 1 in. (2.5 cm.) down the stem as soon as the thinnings are large enough to cook, about late April. Subse-quently every other berry can be picked to provide more culinary fruit, the remainder left to grow on the bush until ripe. This treatment will give ripe fruit up to the size of a large walnut. Yield can be anything from 5–15 lb. per bush, according to soil, age and season.

Propagate and Train

Hardwood cuttings 12 in. (30 cm.) long are taken from the current season's growth. All but the top four or so buds are removed to produce the clean stem or short trunk. Gooseberries do not root quite as easily as currants. Greater success will be achieved if cuttings are taken while there are still leaves on the bushes and the buds are left on until well rooted and the unwanted shoots and dormant eyes re-moved the following winter. Red and white currants and gooseberries are good subjects to train against fences, walls and wires as cordons. A single stem cordon is just like one branch spur pruned. The single lead shoot is pruned back to half its annual growth each year and all side shoots shortened right back to form fruiting spurs. A double cordon is formed by selecting two strong side shoots in the second season from cutt-ings and training these horizon-tally while still green and supple. Once established and outstretched to the length required they are allowed to grow upward to form a "U". Any central lead growth is cut away.

Pests and Diseases

Gooseberry Sawfly caterpillars, green with black spots, eat the leaves right back to the leaf ribs April/May. Control by hand picking off the caterpillars or spraying with Derris or Mala-thion.

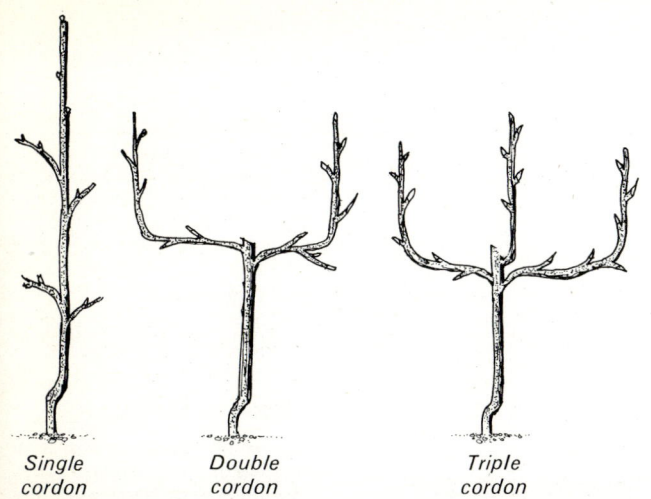

Single
cordon

Double
cordon

Triple
cordon

American Gooseberry Mildew coats leaves, shoots and fruit with a powdery white growth which turns felty and brown.
Soft growth caused by too much nitrogen fertiliser and lack of pruning encourages this disease. Cut out and burn diseased shoots late August. Spray with Dinocap or Benomyl, two or three applications at 7–14 day intervals may be needed.

Note

The old way to control mildew was a spray of 3 oz. of washing soda and $1\frac{1}{2}$ oz. of soft soap to 1 gallon of water.

Grapes

Warm, sunny positions and a very warm summer and autumn are needed for quality dessert grapes to be grown outside in all but the warmest parts of the country. Good crops can, however, be grown for wine outdoors and for dessert under cold glass.

Varieties

'Black Hamburg' is the best variety for cold greenhouses and 'Buckland Sweetwater' and 'Foster's Seedling' are two of several possible white grapes There are a number of varieties suited to outdoor growing, from 'Riesling Sylvaner', suitable for wine and dessert and 'Brant', a small black grape worth growing as much for the brilliant crimson autumn leaf colour as the juicy fruit.

How to Grow

Grapes are deep rooting, long lived and very hardy. They require a free draining soil not over rich. Although very hardy when dormant some protection is needed in spring because the young spring growth can be damaged by late frosts. Grapes grown in cold greenhouses can have the roots outside and the rod (the name given to the vine stem) taken through the base of a side wall and trained up on wires 15–18 in. (38–45 cm.) under the glass. Carefully trained, the gardener can grow grapes either one end or in the roof of a greenhouse, leaving floor space for other crops.

Prepare the soil by digging two spades' depth over an area 3 ft. (0.9 m.) by 5 ft. (1.5 m.), add compost to improve drainage. Pot-grown vines are planted 9 in. (23 cm.) away from walls and 5 ft. (1.5 m.) apart for single rod specimens.

Prune

It is possible to cut the pot grown vine back by two-thirds and train two resulting branches like cordon gooseberries horizontally. Three or four side shoots 3 ft. (0.9 m.) apart are then trained up to form rods This takes several seasons however, and planting three o

four different plants will be easier, quicker, heavier fruiting and allow more than one variety to be grown.

The dormant vine is pruned back to well ripened wood after leaf fall. Each year the lead shoot is pruned back into ripe wood again and trained up until it reaches the required height and/or length. Side shoots develop and these are tied to the horizontal wires. After leaf fall lower the rod so it is horizontal for its length and prune all side shoots (laterals) back to two buds (two leaf stalks along the shoot). Lowering the cane ensures growth all along the rod. New shoots will come from the cut back laterals (spurs) and when growth starts tie the rod up and select one good shoot from each spur. Tie this to a wire when 12 in. (30 cm.) long and pinch the tip of the shoot two leaves past a flower truss. Side shoots from the pinched laterals can be stopped after one leaf if growth becomes excessive in summer. Pruning immediately after leaf fall reduces the chance of the cuts losing sap – called bleeding.

Summer Care

While at no time should roots be either dry or waterlogged a

dry atmosphere midday in May/ June when the flowers open helps pollination. Remove any flowers in the first year. Just draw the half closed fingers down the bunches to help pollination, if you have more than one variety so much the better.

June/July will see flowers set and it is necessary to thin the berries with long pointed scissors, a free setting variety like 'Black Hamburg' will need two thirds of the berries cut off to ensure good large grapes on a nice shapely bunch. Thin out over a period and start as soon as possible because it is easier to do before the berries swell and touch one another.

Do not crop a cane too early, one bunch to a three-year old rod, 4–5 on a 4-year and then up to one bunch to each foot of rod. Berries swell rapidly until the pips start to form July/ August when they appear to stand still for three weeks. Avoid excessive watering and temperature fluctuations at this time.

It is advisable to keep vines freely ventilated early in the year, it prevents too early a start to growth and it subsequently helps reduce the chance of mildew.

Propagation

New plants can be raised by taking hardwood cuttings 12 in. (30 cm.) long after leaf fall. Insert 4–5 in. (10–12 cm.) in soil outside with base in sand.

Harvest

Once ripe, cut bunches on the stalk can be hung in a cool place and stored for several weeks. Remove any rotting berries to prevent the rot spreading.

Outdoor Grapes

Single rod training is simplest and outdoor vines can be given this treatment. The rods can be trained up walls, along fences and horizontal wires supported by posts in the open garden. Mulching to retain moisture in summer is an advantage for all vines and especially those close to walls.

Another training system outside is to cut the young plant hard back in the autumn (to 4 in. (10 cm.)). The following autumn the resulting strong cane is cut back to two leaf scars — two buds — to provide two strong rods in the second year. Cut one of these back to two buds in the third autumn to provide replacement rods and cut the second rod back to seven buds, which will produce fruiting laterals. After fruiting the rod is cut hard back and the new rods tied in its place.

Pests and Diseases

Scale insects and *mealy bug* are controlled by tar oil winter wash applied when the rods are dormant.

Red spider mite will be a problem under glass where the atmosphere is dry. Regular syringing with clear water and damping down the floor reduces this pest and improves growth.

Mildew can be a very serious disease, especially under glass. See that the plants do not get dry at the roots and thin back sub-laterals if the leaves and growth gets too thick. Spray thoroughly with Dinocap when the shoots are 2–3 in. (5–7.5 cm.) long. A second spray when the flowers have set may be needed.

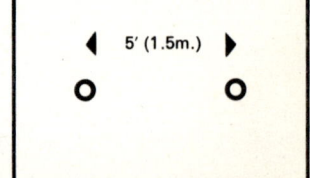

5' (1.5m.)

Pears

The cultivation of pears is very similar to that of apples, flowering two weeks or more earlier than apples and requiring a warmer climate generally, they tend to be planted more in the southern half of England, in sheltered gardens and as trained trees, given the protection of a wall. The vigorous growing young shoots and leaves are soft and all too easily torn and blackened by strong cold winds in spring. They are, however, very worthwhile garden fruits with the bonus of magnificent early blossom in spring.

Varieties

There are very many varieties, one specialist nurseryman offers more than fifty of them and it is to be hoped new gardeners will be tempted to move on with experience from the 10 × 12 plot and this restricted list to a more adventurous selection. 'Conference' is the variety to start with, it will produce fruit without pollination but such fruit may be rather cylindrical in shape. Easy to grow and giving regular heavy crops in all parts of the country, it is ripe in October and can be stored through to Christmas.

Good partners and of even better quality are the September ripening 'Williams' Bon Chrétien', which has upright growth and can be grown in all parts of the country, even against a north wall, and 'Doyenne du Comice', ripe November/January, the most delicious of all pears and excellent to bottle. If Comice is planted in the warmest position it will help bring flowering forward to overlap with Conference and William. Where space prevents the planting of two or three pears, select a "Family Tree". Three varieties on one tree to pollinate one another and provide a success-

Conference

ion of ripe fruits. One family tree well grown will provide sufficient fruit for the average family. Family apple trees are available as well as family pears but unfortunately apples and pears cannot be grown on the same tree.

How to Grow

Avoid chalky soils unless you are prepared to water with sequestrine in spring to prevent yellowing of the leaves. Pears will stand slight waterlogging in winter more than apples but will not resist summer drought so well. All well cultivated garden soils give good results

but where trees flourish and flower but fail to set fruit, either spring frost or inadequate pollination may be the cause.

Most bush and trained trees are grown on E.M. Quince A rootstock which produces compact early fruiting trees. The big standard pear trees seen in old gardens are usually on seedling pear stock. This grows much more vigorously — too big for the average garden — and may take 10–15 years to come into fruit. Hard pruning keeps the tree size down on Quince A stock and spacing is 12 ft. (3.5 m.) apart, vigorous varieties in good soil and lightly pruned needing wider spacing, 15 ft. (4.5 m.).

Trees will grow best where the soil under them is kept cultivated. Mulching with compost in spring is an advantage, as is the application of a general fertiliser at 2–3 oz. (57–85 gm.) per sq. yd. (sq. m.) in January. A little more nitrogen is required by pears compared with apples and 1 oz. (28 gm.) of sulphate of ammonia in spring is wise for trees in grass.

Pruning

Pears require similar treatment to apples, although they respond better to really hard pruning, even to the point of cutting lead shoots of established trees back to 2 in. (5 cm.) each winter and all laterals to 1 in. (2.5 cm.). It will be necessary to reduce the number of fruiting spurs if established trees are carrying too many small fruit. Light pruning will encourage earlier fruiting but heavily laden branches are likely to bend outwards and may need cutting hard back when too low and replacing by the side shoots which will grow away strongly just below the cut. Some 7–10 upright branches will be the aim for closely planted bush trees.

Harvest

Pears are picked when ripe *but before* they soften. When the fruits separate easily from the tree, by just lifting through 90° in the hand, is the time to gather. Flavour and smell develop better if the fruit is stored in single layers in trays or boxes in a cool damp atmosphere. Once the skins have yellowed and before the fruit goes too soft, bring indoors in the warm for a few days to ripen to juicy perfection. Over a period of years a good tree is likely to average 20–30 lb. (9–13.5 kg.) of fruit each season.

Doyenne du Comice

Pests and Diseases

Aphis — several kinds of aphis including greenfly and blackfly cause a black sticky mould over leaves and shoots in spring and summer. Tar oil winter wash, followed by a greenfly spray after the petals have fallen, will control this disease.

Pear midge occurs occasionally and if it does will reappear year after year until sprayed. Symptoms are the failure of small fruits to develop, they turn black and fall. Several white maggots will be found inside infected fruits. Cultivating the soil under trees exposes this pest to predators and spraying at white flower bud stage with dimethoate gives control.

Pear leaf blister produces blisters pale green or pink, turning brown on the leaves from April onwards. Small attacks are best controlled by removing and burning infected leaves. Lime sulphur — which also controls scab — applied late March as the buds begin to open gives control (Lime sulphur cannot be used on Comice).

Pear scab black scabs and cracks on fruit, light green spots on the leaves which turn brown and blistered, spotted young shoots, are all symptoms of this disease. Warm, humid conditions speed the spread of this disease and several sprays with fungicides like captan will be needed to control it. Collect and burn diseased leaves and prune out diseased shoots.

Fireblight sudden total blackening of young shoots as if burnt by fire and not to be confused with the more bruising, blackening effect of wind, and exudation and liquid streaks running down the bark of branches is caused by this bacterial disease. Report this disease to your local Ministry of Agriculture office. All infected wood has to be cut out and burned, the tools subsequently sterilised.

Williams Bon Chretien

12′ (3.5m.)

45

Peaches and Nectarines

Peaches can be grown satis-factorily outside as bush trees in the south of the country and in warm sheltered gardens. Trained as fan trees against south or west facing walls, they will thrive and fruit as far north as Yorkshire and the West of Scotland. Elsewhere fan trees under cold glass fruit well. Nectarines are a smooth skin-ned form of peach but not quite so hardy and best grown as fans in a protected situation.

Varieties

While trees grown from pips will sometimes fruit satisfactor-ily, named varieties grafted onto the dwarfing 'St. Julien A' stock should be planted in small gardens. The early August fruit-ing peach 'Peregrine' and nectarine 'Lord Napier' were raised by Rivers in Britain 1906 and 1869 respectively and have proved reliable. Peach 'Roch-ester' is a good variety for bush cultivation. All varieties are self pollinating and it is better to plant one than two in a small garden to avoid excessive pruning.

How to Grow

Bare root trees are best planted October/November and early spring, container grown trees at any time. Well cultivated garden soil, not too chalky, is best, it needs to be free draining but water retentive in summer. This is best achieved by adding plenty of well rotted compost when digging thoroughly ahead of planting, this is especially important against walls and fences.

Water well in very dry weather, dust the open flowers midday with a feather or soft paint brush when dry and sunny to help pollination. Gently misting with water on sunny days also helps fruit set. When the peaches are the size of a penny single them out and when the size of a 10 pence piece thin to 9 in. (23 cm.) apart.

Prune

Bush trees with the branch framework established require little pruning. Cut out any diseased and dead wood in May. At this time occasionally prune back a branch to en-courage new growth from the centre of the tree.

Fan trees take time to train and develop but are well worth the effort. Trained trees purchased from the nursery have the basic branch framework (see page 10–11) and it is a matter of pruning the lead shoots of each branch back in early spring, ideally to a cluster of three buds at one point – you will see what I mean when looking at the stem – to get two or three new branches radiating out from the cut. Like the ribs of an umbrella increasing as the branches radiate out from the centre trunk.

Once branches extend to the area of wall or fence available

attention is directed exclusively to fruiting wood. Flower and fruit are produced on the previous year's wood, plump rounded buds being flower buds and the longer, thinner buds producing growth. All shoots growing toward the wall or at 90° away from it are rubbed out in April while young, soft and green. Select shoots on top and under side of each branch, every 6 in. (15 cm.) or so along it and tie those to the horizontal support wires, which need to be 9 in. (23 cm.) apart. These side-shoots need to be no closer than 4 in. (10 cm.) when tied in and surplus shoots are pinched back to four leaves. The side-shoots have the tip pinched out when 18 in. (45 cm.) long, it is these laterals which bear fruit. Each year a strong new shoot is trained from the base of the lateral alongside as replacement when the fruited branch is cut out in late summer. Surplus shoots are either pinched back to four leaves or rubbed out altogether.

Harvest

Ease off syringing the foliage with water as the fruits start to ripen and tie leaves back to allow sun to get to the fruits. Once the flesh softens to touch around the stalk the fruits can be gathered and spaced on tissue in a cool place, will store for several weeks.

Pests and Diseases

Aphis is controlled with tar oil in winter and greenfly sprays in summer.
Glasshouse red spider mite is best controlled by repeated syringing and damping down paths with water at least twice a day, morning and evening. This helps growth as well as reducing spider. See that the plants are not dry at the root. A yellowish-bronzing of the leaves is typical of red spider attack. Azobenzine smokes can be used under glass. Collect and burn all fallen leaves.
Mildew also comes with dry soils, once seen routine sulphur sprays at 14-day intervals will control.
Peach leaf curl causes red blisters and curled leaves, spray with lime sulphur or copper fungicide in January/February when buds begin to swell, again 10 days later and before flower buds open and as the leaves fall in the autumn.

20' (6.1 m.)

Plums, Gages and Damsons

An apple tree would be my first choice for the small garden and the plum 'Victoria' next. There can be no more useful fruit than plums and gages, delicious eaten fresh from the tree when ripe and suitable for many culinary purposes, especially stewed, for pies, bottled and for jams.

Varieties

Once again many varieties are available from the specialist nurseryman, each one having specific qualities. Selected here are a cross section of the different types, choosing the easiest and most popular. All except 'Cambridge Gage' are self pollinating although in common with other fruits better crops will often be achieved if cross pollinating occurs. First choice must be 'Victoria', ripe to eat fresh in late August/early September but suitable for cooking a little earlier. A good tree to fan train and although self pollinating,

because of mid season flowering cross pollinates with plums, damsons and gages. 'Czar' is a reliable early purple/black culinary plum of upright hardy growth, 'Marjorie's Seedling' is a large culinary plum ripe in October to eat from the tree. Gages have that rather special flavour, with 'Cambridge Gage' a more free fruiting variety of the 'Old Greengage', of greenish colour and yellow, flushed red when ripe. While these greengages grow well, they do not fruit regularly and a variety like 'Oullin's Gage' (which pollinates Cambridge') is a better choice. It is a golden gage plum suitable for eating and cooking. Finally the rich flavour of damson provided by Prune Damson (also known as 'Shropshire Prune'), a compact upright growing tree, and the larger more spreading 'Merryweather'.

How to Grow

Heavy, wet soils and very acid soils are not suitable, both can be improved, however, by cultivation, adding plenty of well rotted compost and lime to acid soils. Avoid frost hollows because spring frosts when the early flowers open cause loss of crop for that year. Fan trained trees against walls can be netted to protect from bullfinches taking buds in winter and giving some protection from frost.

Plums and gages are better given space, warm sunny situations and weather will give the best fruit. Select damsons for areas of high rainfall. The best rootstock for small gardens is the semi dwarfing St. Julien A and varieties on this stock should start to fruit when 3–4 years old. They need spacing 12 ft. (3.5 m.) apart. Trees on the more vigorous Brompton

and Myrobalan stocks will yield more heavily but need spacing 18–20 ft. (5.5–6 m.) apart.

A good heavy mulch of manure and well rotted compost will improve the performance of these fruits. Yields will vary tremendously according to weather but a well grown 'Victoria' should yield 40 lb. (18 kg.) or more each year for a bush tree and 15 lb. (6.8 kg.) for a fan.

Prune

Nurserymen usually supply two and three-year old trees which already have the basic branch framework established. It is as well to leave unpruned in the first year or just tip trees transplanted bare root, and in the second spring — the first spring for container grown trees which have not suffered root disturbance — cut the lead shoots which will grow to form main branches back by half. Little subsequent pruning will be necessary save on rather strong growing lead shoots of varieties like 'Victoria' which can be shortened back in spring to avoid producing long weeping branches.

Pruning of mature trees is best undertaken in June/August period and all wounds covered with proprietary tree wound paste to prevent silver leaf disease entry.

Fan trained trees on St. Julien A rootstock and planted 15 ft. (4.5 m.) apart are pruned like peaches to form the branch framework. Much of this has been done with fan trees purchased from the garden centre. Side shoots growing at right angles to the wall are rubbed out while young and green. Other laterals are tied in to the horizontal support wires like peaches and surplus side shoots stopped by pinching out the tip after seven leaves have formed. Fruiting on old and new wood, the fruiting wood is left in and *not* pruned back as we do for peaches. After fruiting prune back the 7-leaf long shoots by half and cut out any thin and unwanted branches. Very strong upward growing shoots from the centre of the fan are best removed as these will take all the vigour from the fan.

Harvest

Where fruits are too small, thin out in June or July to leave fruit every 2 in. (5 cm.) along the branch. This is the way to get large quality dessert plums. For eating fresh the fruit is best picked over several times, selecting fully ripe fruit. Earlier gathering is acceptable for cooking purposes and helps extend the season.

Pests and Disease

Aphis can be a nuisance causing black sooty mould on the leaves and fruit. Tar oil in winter and pre and post blossom greenfly killers like formothion will control.

Birds netting is essential in many gardens to prevent bullfinches eating dormant buds in winter and other birds pecking ripe fruit.

Silver leaf disease not only causes silver colour in the leaves but also purplish brown staining in the wood. If pared down with a knife this browning is clearly seen. All wood which has died back as a result of this disease must be cut out, cut back past the inner staining by July and the wound painted over to prevent re-infection. The fungus spores which spread are released from *dead* wood.

Bush on dwarf stock

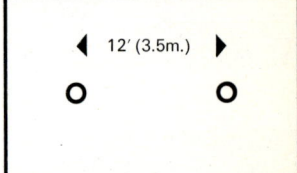

12' (3.5m.)

Bush on vigorous stock

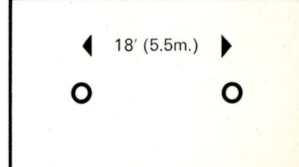

18' (5.5m.)

Fan

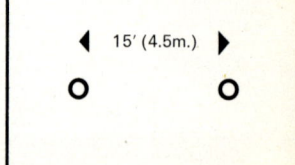

15' (4.5m.)

Quince

Quince is best planted as a large ornamental shrub rather than a specimen fruit. It will make a nice rounded bush some 12 ft. (3.5 m.) in diameter with attractive foliage, dark green above, light greyish-green beneath, turning gold in the autumn, white or rose pink flowers 2 in. (5 cm.) across in May are followed by golden fruits. These fruits can be stewed and used to make quince cheese, jam and jelly.

Varieties

'Vranja' (illus.) is the most widely offered variety and has attractive flowers and plump, rounded fruits. It will start to flower and fruit in the second year. All varieties are self fertile.

How to Grow

North of York and away from the west coast of Scotland, the protection of a south facing wall is best to ensure ripening of fruits in the autumn. All well cultivated garden soils are suitable including rather wet situations. Once planted and established they require little attention.

Prune

Just thin out branches in winter occasionally if growth becomes very thick. It is better not to prune hard or try to train this fruit.

Harvest

Fruits need to be gathered in early October, before the chance of frost. Kept in a cool place they continue to ripen and will store for a couple of months. It is as well to store away from other fruits which are liable to pick up the strong aroma coming from the quince.

Propagation

New plants are grown from hardwood cuttings 12 in. (30 cm.) long inserted into soil in November.

Pests and Diseases

Similar problems to those found affecting apples and pears affect quince and are controlled in the same way.
Brown Rot. Fruits turn brown, often spreading out from bird peck or similar damage and eventually concentric rings of white fungus spores appear. Diseased fruits may fall or just shrivel and remain on the tree. This disease can also enter shoots to cause cankers and die-back. Collect and burn all diseased fruit and see that storage trays and shelves are scrubbed out with soda and hot water before re-use.

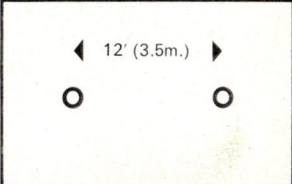

12' (3.5m.)

Raspberries

Second only to strawberries in the small garden raspberries reign supreme. They are the best of all fruits for deep freezing, swift to fruit, unbeatable for dessert and culinary purposes.

Varieties

MID SEASON kinds, the best known June/July fruiting including 'Malling Promise', early and heavy cropping, 'Malling Jewel', a heavy and regular cropper mid-season and easy to pick. 'Glen Clova' has large fruits of good flavour which start to ripen early and crop over a long period. 'Malling Admiral' is somewhat later cropping and 'Delight' has very large, easily picked fruit. One of the heaviest cropping and resistant to pests and diseases. *AUTUMN FRUITING* kinds fruit from September to the frost. 'September' is best known with red fruits but 'Zeva' crops longer and heavily, from July to the frost, with large red fruits of excellent quality. Select this variety to grow canes in tubs. Two recently introduced varieties from America which look to be worth watching are 'Fallgold' with sweet golden yellow fruit and 'Heritage', said to be an improvement on 'Zeva'.

How to Grow

All well cultivated garden soils are suitable and most sites, including partially shaded ones. Waterlogging in the winter must be avoided. The addition of well rotted compost with preparatory digging and subsequently as a mulch, to provide a cool moist root run near the surface in summer increases the crop. Relatively late flowering, spring frost damage is unlikely.

Be sure the soil is clear of perennial weeds before planting because canes will crop for 8–10 years once established. Bare root canes are best planted in November but can be transplanted any time from November to late March as long as the soil is not frozen. Container grown, they can be planted at any time, even in fruit.

Always plant 'certified' disease-free stock, it is not worth saving at the outset on self saved canes to have reduced yields because of virus diseases over a number of years. Plant firmly 15–18 in. (38–45 cm.) apart, if more than one row is planted allow 4–6 ft. (1.2–1.8 m.) between rows. Rows tend to get wider as they age and the wider spacing is necessary for long term crops on rich soil.

Weed control is best effected by heavy mulching with well rotted manure and/or compost. Try not to dig close to the surface rooting raspberries as this will reduce growth and subsequent crop. Whilst autumn fruiting varieties are virtually self supporting, the summer fruiting kinds will require support. New canes are tied to wires 3½ ft. (1 m.) and 5 ft. (1.5 m.) high, the wires secured to stakes.

Pruning

Bare root canes are cut back to 6–9 in. (15–23 cm.) above soil level after planting. New canes grow the following summer and these are tied to the wires to fruit 15–18 months from planting. Container grown canes will crop lightly the first summer after planting. All fruited canes are pruned out in August and new canes are tied to the wires. Select enough new canes to tie one every 3–4 in. (7.5–10 cm.) along the wire, cut out any surplus.

Autumn fruiting varieties are cut back after planting bare root canes. They are *not* pruned in

August but fruited wood is left until the following *February* when it is cut to the ground. The roots then produce new canes which fruit the same year.

Harvest

Gather as ripe by gently pulling fruit from the "plug" which stays behind on the cane. Some varieties come away from the plug more easily than others. Each 1 ft. (30 cm.) of row is likely to yield 1 lb. (454 gm.) of fruit. A 10 ft. (3 m.) row in poor soil under the shade of a pear tree yielded 5 lb. 2 oz. (2.31 kg) in the heat of mid June/early July, 1976. Autumn fruiting varieties crop over a longer period but not so heavily in total. Plenty of water and liquid fertiliser as fruits start to swell increases yield and strengthens canes for next season's crop.

Pests and Disease

Raspberry Beetle causes small maggots in ripe fruit, spray or dust with derris or malathion when the first pink fruit is seen to control.

Cane spot, first seen May/June as small purple spots which turn grey with purple edge and *Spur Blight*, purple blotches in August which turn silver and cause die-back are controlled with sprays of benomyl.

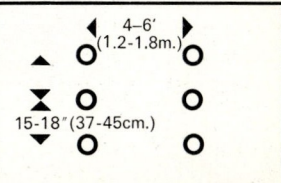

Rhubarb — outdoors

Not really a fruit or a vegetable but one of the easiest plants to grow and one of the most productive in a garden.

Varieties

'Timperley Early' is an excellent variety for gardens, early growing and good for outdoor and indoor forcing purposes. 'Prince Albert' is another early variety. 'The Sutton' and 'Victoria' will yield more stems but are later and not suitable for early forcing, they do, however, crop well into the summer.

How to Grow

All garden soils are suitable with best crops from those with plenty of well rotted compost to retain moisture. While rhubarb grows anywhere, try to find an open sunny site. Space the plants – usually called crowns – $2\frac{1}{2}$–3 feet (75 cm.–1 m.) apart where they will establish and crop for many years.

Apply Growmore or other general fertiliser at 4 oz. per square yard (m²) before planting and each subsequent spring. The addition of well rotted compost in spring each year helps retain moisture and improves growth.

Prune

Just cut out flower stems when they develop and remove old dead leaves in the winter tidy-up.

Harvest

Leave the crown in the first year to build strength, then pull a few stems the second year before cropping more heavily in the third and successive years, from early February to August. Try always to leave three or four good leaves on each plant to continue building up the strength of the plant. For the heaviest yield just pull fully grown stems without allowing them to get old. Old stems are 'stringy' when snapped in half. One strong crown will yield 6–11 lb. a year.

Propagate

Named varieties by lifting two and three-year old established plants in February/March and cut them up in pieces with a spade. Each piece – called a set or crown – must have at least one good rounded bud on a piece of root the size of two fists one on top of the other.

Notes

Cover with box filled with straw for earlier growth.

Rhubarb — for forcing

Succulent young pink stems forced into growth early make a delicious fresh winter sweet.

Varieties

like 'Timperley Early' can be forced earlier and will produce much earlier crops.

How to Grow

Two and three-year old plants are the easiest to handle. They are grown in the open garden and can be spaced 2 ft. (60 cm.) apart if lifted in the 2nd or 3rd year. Lift in the autumn and leave on the surface to expose them to cold temperatures. Mid November in the north and late November/early December in the south is the earliest early varieties can be brought indoors. Crowns need periods of cold to equal winter before we can fool them into thinking spring has arrived by taking them into the warm. Late varieties need more cold before forcing from mid January.

When lifting be careful not to knock off any thick thongy roots. The greater the weight of root retained the greater weight of forced stems produced. Pack damp peat, soil or similar material around the roots, keep them dark and warm, 50–55°F (10°C) and forced stems will be ready to pull in about a month. Placing the crown in a black polythene bag is an easy way to force.

Harvest

Forced stems are mature when the pale lemon leaf colour starts to darken, try to pull just before this darkening occurs and the leaf edges go brown. Pull rhubarb by slipping the index finger well down the stem and pressing outwards while grasping and pulling to remove the whole stem cleanly from the crown. Discard the roots after forcing.

Propagation

It is also possible to raise rhubarb from seed sown outdoors in spring. Do not pull from seed raised plants for at least two years. Plants from seed will be variable in growth, yield and earliness.

Pests and Diseases

None to worry about — occasionally greenfly or caterpillars may occur and are easily controlled with garden insecticides.

Strawberries

Every household should try to grow a few strawberries. If the only space you have is a foot or two of window sill, succulent red berries in late April/early May are possible. Outside on a paved area we can grow them in pots, boxes, fertilised peat filled bags and in tubs or towers. The smallest plot will also carry a row to produce fruit either in mid summer or from June to the frost. There are three main types, the best known and of greatest import-ance are the ordinary summer fruiting cultivars, the next are the "perpetuals" and finally the alpine strawberries.

Varieties

Summer (June–July) *Fruiting* (illus. p. 56)
There are many to choose from and any one will give good crops. Be sure to buy 'certified, that is guaranteed virus disease free plants at the beginning. 'Cambridge Favourite' is the most widely grown commercial variety, easy to grow, heavy cropping and ideal for jams and freezing. 'Cambridge Vigour' — very good flavour and an excel-lent cultivar to crop one year. 'Grandee' — see illustration of fruit grown in my garden (p. 56) — produces massive berries up to 3 in. across, that is as large as a Cox's apple; a startling variety which crops heavily and is of reasonable flavour.
'Pantagruella' is a new variety I am watching, it is said to be 14 days earlier than the previously mentioned kinds, has upright leaves and can be planted as close as 6 in. (15 cm.) apart. 'Redgauntlet' is a good cropper and if covered by cloches to crop early, and old leaves stripped off after fruiting, it will produce a second autumn crop.

'Royal Sovereign' is well flavoured but rather light cropping and not easy to grow. 'Tamella' produces large early fruits in the first year, very heavy yielding and a good all-round variety.

Perpetual (June-October)
Fruiting (illus. p. 57)
'Gento' is the variety I find most successful so far. The parent plant and its runners flower and fruit with the main crop August to October. It fruits well into the autumn with cloche and similar protection. 'Rabunda' crops heavily and has bright red fruit. The so called "climbing strawberries" are usually varieties from this group and it is more a matter of tying up the runners against some form of trellis rather than the strawberries climbing! If you wish to have a go at this then 'Trellisa' is the variety.

Alpine Strawberry

'Baron Solemacher' is the best known variety and a near relative of the true alpine strawberry. It is also listed under the perpetual fruiters, with fingernail sized berries carried from June to the frost. Raised from seed it crops the same year from an early spring sowing. The fruit is rather small and the woody seeds rather large!

How to Grow

All well cultivated garden soils are suitable and those improved by the addition of well rotted compost will crop that much more heavily. A sunny position is best but they will crop in some shade. Strawberries can be planted in late summer,

autumn and spring. Remember, every week later than the middle of August for planting summer fruiting varieties of bare root plants means the loss of 1 oz. (28 gm.) of fruit the next summer. Late autumn and spring planted bare root plants are better with the blooms removed in May to build strength for future seasons' heavy crops. Plants fruiting on maiden (one-year old) plants will bear the earliest and the largest fruits. In subsequent years, there will be more fruit and a heavier yield but somewhat later and smaller berries. Pot grown runners can be planted later than mid August and because they have no root disturbance will fruit well the following June, like early planted bare root runners. Set the runners 12–18 in. (30–45 cm.) apart in the row and 2 ft. (60 cm.) between rows if the rows are to be down for 4–5 years.

One easy way with strawberries is to plant a single row, fairly close in the row, crop it the first summer and take at least one good runner from each plant to form a new row and then dig the fruited row in. This prevents perennial weeds getting established, masses of runners rooting everywhere and the strawberry becomes a one year rotation in the vegetable plot.

Black polythene mulching – or any other colour polythene come to that – is the easiest way with strawberries. Strips of polythene 2 ft. (60 cm.) wide are placed down the row. Potting compost and peat bags slit down both sides are excellent. Make two drills in the soil 9 in. (23 cm.) each side of where the strawberry plants will go, as if you were sowing seeds, and put the edge of the polythene in the drill and pull back soil to bury the edges.

This will give an 18 in. strip of polythene across the garden; cut crosses in the polythene and plant your runners through the holes. The strawberries grow well through the polythene which supresses weeds, keeps the fruit clean, stops runners rooting everywhere and gives up to 5 years work-free strawberry cropping (see illus. p. 58). Polythene other than black will probably break down in the sunlight after 3 or 4 years.

When planting the base of the leaf stalk should be at soil level. The "crown" of the plant just at surface level also, do not plant too deep or too shallow, but plant firmly.

Runners on summer fruiting kinds are pinched off as soon as they appear unless you want to save one or two for a new planting. Runners on perpetual fruiting varieties are left to flower and fruit; it is as well to remove flowers on perpetuals the first May following planting to allow strength to build for heavy autumn cropping. All flowers are allowed to fruit in the second year.

Liquid fertiliser, tomato fertiliser is excellent, as the berries start to swell increases fruit size and helps build the plant ready for the next flush.

Harvesting

Traditionally straw is used to cover the soil and prevent dirt splashing up over the fruit. Polythene sheet is easier and cleaner for the small suburban garden. Pick the fruit on the stalk as it ripens.

Propagation

One or two runners can be rooted from each plant in July. It is advisable to keep the stock young and vigorous for heavy crops. Dig in all your plants every five or six years and have a fresh start with certified disease-free stock. Such stock is ideal to produce more rooted runners in the July after planting. Just peg the biggest runner close to the plant into $3\frac{1}{2}$ in. (9 cm.) pots of potting compost. Once well rooted they can be cut from the parent and moved to the permanent fruiting site.

Pests and Diseases

Aphis, sticky leaves are a sure sign of this pest and greenfly killers will quickly remove them. *Slugs* and *snails* can eat the fruit, especially in wet seasons, and Methiocarb slug pellets will control them and straw-

berry seed beetle which eats the seeds on the fruit. Sprinkle some Methiocarb pellets on the soil before covering with polythene sheet mulch and fruit protector.

Botrytis commonly called "grey mould", the disease which causes fruit to go brown and rotten, the brown subsequently covered with a furry grey mould. One of the fungicides like benomyl, will control. Cloche covering to keep fruit dry also helps.

Early Crops

Covering rows of strawberries in early spring with cloches gives protection to the flowers from early spring frost. (A sure sign of frost damage is the yellow centre of the flower going black). They also give earlier fruits and protection from birds. Glass cloches are good but need careful handling and are not advisable in gardens where children play ball! The best cloches and easiest to handle are made of clear and long lasting P.V.C. sheets supported by wire frames.

Cheapest and very easy to use once you have the knack are polythene tunnel cloches. Here

Inside view of Polythene tunnel cloche

Polythene tunnel cloche

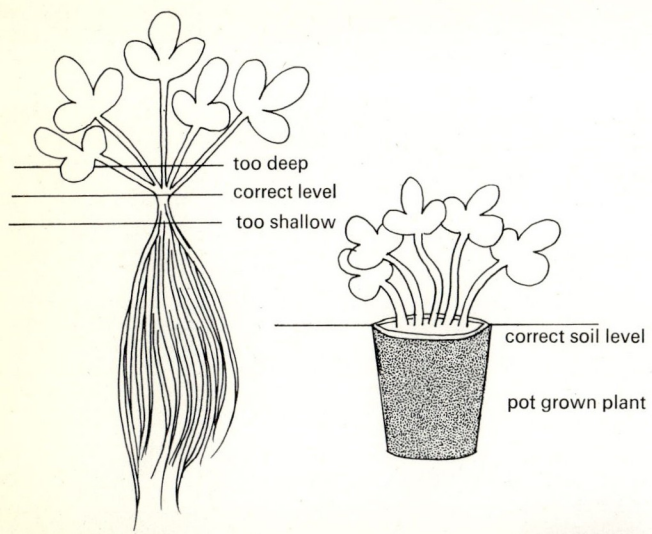

too deep
correct level
too shallow

correct soil level

pot grown plant

wire hoops are pushed into the ground at 3 ft. (1 m.) intervals down the row, with loops in the wire at ground level. A long strip of polythene is put over the hoops and the ends either buried in the soil or tied to stakes (see illus. p. 58). A retaining wire goes from the loop on one side, over the polythene sheet to the loop on the other side, keeping the polythene taut and in place. You can get at the strawberries by just lifting up one edge of the polythene between the two wires. It is worth leaving the polythene up on sunny days when plants are in flower to help pollination.

Window sill growing

Half pots 6 in. (15 cm.) diameter are ideal for indoor culture (see illus.). Using all peat potting compost pot up runners in early August. Leave outdoors until February then bring in and grow like house plants. Tickle the flowers which are marguerite coloured with a feather when in full bloom to pollinate and by late April you can be picking succulent ripe berries. Inadequate pollination causes mis-shapen fruits. Each pot will yield 4-6 oz. (113-170 gm.).

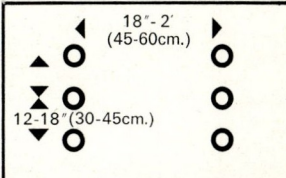

18″- 2′
(45-60cm.)

12-18″(30-45cm.)

Soft Fruit: Pest and Disease Control Chart

Problem	Spray	Mar	Apl	May	Jun	Jly	Aug	Notes
DISEASES								
BOTRYTIS (Greymould) Strawberries and cane fruit	benomyl, or dichlofluanid, or thiophanate-methyl, or thiram				●——	——●		2 or 3 sprays at 14-day intervals.
CANE SPOT Rasps, logans and hybrid berries	benomyl, or thiophanate-methyl, or thiram			●——	——	——●		2 or 3 sprays at 14-day intervals
LEAF SPOT Black, red and white currants	benomyl, or thiophanate-methyl, or thiram			●——	——	——●		2 or 3 sprays at 14-day intervals
MILDEW (American gooseberry mildew) Gooseberries, Blackcurrants	benomyl, or dinocap, or thiophanate-methyl			●				
SPUR BLIGHT Logans, Rasps.	benomyl, or thiophanate-methyl, or thiram	●——	——	——●				2 or 3 sprays at 14-day intervals. Start when shoots are ½ in (1cm) long
PESTS								
APHIS (Greenfly) All soft fruit	malathion or dimethoate or fenitrothion or formothion or rotenone	●——	——	——	——	——●		tar oil Dec./Jan. all but strawberries
BIG BUD MITE Blackcurrants	lime sulphur		●——	——●				some varieties are damaged by this sulphur spray
CAPSID Currants	malathion or bioresmethrin or dimethoate or fenitrothion or pirimiphos-methyl			●——	——	——●		
RASPBERRY BEETLE Cane fruit	fenitrothion, or malathion, or pirimiphos-methyl, or rotenone				●——	——●		
SAWFLY (and other caterpillars) Gooseberries	malathion, or bioresmethrin, or fenitrothion or pirimiphos-methyl, or rotenone			●——	——	——●		

NOTE: Combined sprays, for example malathion/benomyl, or fenitrothion/thiophanate-methyl in May will control most problems. Spray at the first sign of attack and when weather is still — usually evenings. Dust when dew is on plants to help chemicals to stick. Avoid using the same chemical year after year, to avoid build up of resistance. See page 63 for the guide to some brand names.

Top Fruit: Pest and Disease Control Chart

Problem	Spray	Feb	Mar	Apl	May	Jun	Jly	Aug	Notes
PESTS									
APHID (Greenfly) Apples, Pear, Plum, Cherry. (Blackfly) Peach	bioresmethrin or dimethoate or formothion or malathion or menazon or pirimicarb or pirimiphos-methyl, or resmethrin or rotenone or diazinon			⊢——————⊣					Dec/Jan Tar oil.
WOOLLY APHID Apple	menazon, or HCH or dimethoate of malathion				⊢——⊣				green to pink flower bud stage. Before May
CAPSID Apple	bioresmethrin, or fenitrothion or HCH or malathion or pirimiphos-methyl			⊢—⊣					
CATERPILLAR (Winter Moth and Sawfly) Apple	trichlorphon or fenitrothion or HCH or pirimiphos-methyl								grease band apply September Also for Tortrix Caterpillar
CODLING MOTH Apple	fenitrothion, or HCH or malathion or pirimiphos-methyl				⊢——————⊣				
LEAF BLISTER MITE Pears	5% lime sulphur	⊢—⊣							
MIDGE PEAR	dimethoate or fenitrothion or HCH			⊢——⊣					
RED SPIDER MITE Apples, plum, etc.	diazinon, malathion or dinocap or pirimiphos-methyl or rotenone	⊢————————⊣							White flower bud stage DNOC/pet. February. Not a problem on unsprayed trees, natural predators control
GLASSHOUSE RED SPIDER MITE Peaches	diazinon, dimethoate, malathion, pirimiphos-methyl or rotenone			⊢————————⊣					
DISEASES									
CANKER Apples	liquid copper	⊢—⊣							1 spray ½ leaf fall 1 spray at leaf fall
LEAF BLIGHT Quince	liquid copper								
LEAF CURL Peaches	lime sulphur or liquid copper. thiram or zineb	⊢—⊣							And at leaf fall 7–14 day intervals
MILDEW Apples, Quince	dinocap or benomyl or thiophanate-methyl		⊢——————————⊣						7–14 day intervals
MILDEW Peach	sulphur or benomyl or thiophanate-methyl								
SCAB Apples, pears	benomyl or captan or thiram or zineb or thiophanate-methyl		⊢————————⊣						as soon as seen

NOTES: Do not spray with chemicals which harm bees when plants are in flower. Change choice of chemical to avoid build up of resistant strains of pest and disease.

Garden Chemicals

ACTIVE CHEMICAL	COMMON NAME	PROPRIETARY NAMES
Pesticides		
bioresmethrin (0)		Combat Vegetable Insecticide (Fisons), Combat Whitefly (Fisons)
BHC (now HCH) (14)	Lindane	Lindex (Murphy) also in Hexyl Plus (PBI), Abol X (ICI), Combat Garden Insecticide (Fisons)
diazinon (14)		Gesal Garden Insecticide (Airwick (UK)) Combat Soil Insecticide (Fisons)
dicofol		In Combined Pest and Disease Spray (Murphy) (14)
dimethoate (7)	rogor	In Combat Garden Insecticide (Fison), Systemic Insecticide (Murphy)
fenitrothion (14)		Fentro (Murphy)
formothion (7) (not on cherries)		Systemic Liquid (PBI)
malathion (1)		Malathion Greenfly Killer (PBI), Liquid Malathion (Murphy), in Combat Garden and Vegetable Insecticide (Fison)
menazon (14)		Abol-X (ICI)
metaldehyde (0)	slug bait	Many brands
methiocarb (7)		Draza (May and Baker), Slug guard (PBI)
oxydemeton-methyl (21)	metasystox	Greenfly (Aphid) Gun (May and Baker)
pirimicarb (14)		Rapid (ICI) (harmless to lacewings, ladybirds and bees.)
pirimiphos-methyl (7)		Sybol 2 (ICI)
resmethrin (0)		Sprayday (PBI)
rotenone (1)	derris	Abol Derris Dust (ICI), Liquid Derris (PBI)
tar distillate	tar oil	Mortegg (Murphy)
trichlorphon (2)		Dipterex (May and Baker), Kilsect (PBI)
	grease bands	Boltac Greasebands (PBI)
Fungicides		
benomyl (0)	benlate	Benlate (PBI)
captan (0)		Orthocide (Murphy)
copper (0)		Liquid Copper Fungicide (Murphy)
dichlofluanid (21)		Elvaron (May and Baker)
dinocap (7)		Dinocap Mildew Fungicide (Murphy)
dithiocarbamate type	thiram (7) (do not use on fruit to be preserved)	Garden Fungicide (ICI) in Hexyl Plus (PBI), Ovamort Special (Murphy)
DNOC/Petroleum Oil	(watch for varieties susceptible to damage)	
lime sulphur (0)		
thiophanate-methyl (0)		Systemic Fungicide (Murphy)
zineb (7)	dithane	Dithane (PBI)
Wound Paint		
	bitumen	Arbrex (PBI)

Numbers in brackets indicate 'safe harvest interval' (that is days between spraying and picking to eat).

ALWAYS FOLLOW MANUFACTURERS INSTRUCTIONS TO THE LETTER These lists and the help of your local specialist garden sundries retailer, who will recommend equally suitable alternative brands, should provide all the information and products you will need. A full list of the proprietary brands and common names will be found in The British Agrochemicals Association, Directory of Garden Chemicals 1977 edition price 50p from B.A.A.,

SOME USEFUL FIGURES: 1 pint = 20 fluid ounces. 1 fluid ounce = 8 drams; 8 teaspoonsful; 2 tablespoonsful. 1 pint = 568 millilitres. 1 fluid ounce = 28 millilitres. 8 pints = 1 gallon = 4.55 litres. 50 millilitres = 1.75 fluid ounces. 1 litre = 1.75 pints.